100 WALKS IN
Oxfordshire & Berkshire

compiled by

LES MAPLE

The Crowood Press

First published in 1997 by
The Crowood Press Ltd
Ramsbury
Marlborough
Wiltshire SN8 2HR

British Library Cataloguing-in-Publication Data
A catalogue record for this book is
available from the British Library

ISBN 1 86126 026 1

All maps by Janet Powell

Typeset by Carreg Limited, Ross-on-Wye, Herefordshire

Printed in Great Britain by J W Arrowsmith Limited, Bristol

CONTENTS

35.	West Ilsley	$4^1/_2$m	($7^1/_4$km)
36.	Mortimer	$4^1/_2$m	($7^1/_4$km)
37.	Donnington Castle	$4^1/_2$m	($7^1/_4$km)
38.	Wroxton	$4^1/_2$m	($7^1/_4$km)
39.	… and longer version	6m	($9^1/_2$km)
40.	Cottisford	$4^1/_2$m	($6^3/_4$km)
41.	Pangbourne	$4^1/_2$m	($7^1/_4$km)
42.	Goring Heath	$4^1/_2$m	($7^1/_4$km)
43.	Chadlington	$4^1/_2$m	($7^1/_4$km)
44.	Minster Lovell	$4^1/_2$m	($7^1/_4$km)
45.	Aldermaston Wharf and Village	$4^3/_4$m	($7^3/_4$km)
46.	Grey's Court	$4^3/_4$m	($7^1/_2$km)
47.	Bradfield	$4^3/_4$m	($7^3/_4$km)
48.	Bladon and Begbroke	$4^3/_4$m	($7^3/_4$km)
49.	Leckhampstead	$4^3/_4$m	($7^1/_2$km)
50.	Newbridge	$4^3/_4$m	($7^3/_4$km)
51.	Lower Heyford	$4^3/_4$m	($7^3/_4$km)
52.	Hungerford	$4^3/_4$m	($7^3/_4$km)
53.	North Leigh Roman Villa	5m	(8km)
54.	Pishill	5m	(8km)
55.	Stonor Park	5m	(8km)
56.	Brimpton	5m	(8km)
57.	Blenheim Park	5m	(8km)
58.	Hethe	5m	(8km)
59.	Stanford in the Vale	5m	(8km)
60.	Churchill	5m	(8km)
61.	Henley	5m	(8km)
62.	Aldworth	5m	(8km)
63.	… and longer version	$6^1/_2$m	($10^1/_2$km)
64.	Mapledurham	$5^1/_4$m	($8^1/_2$km)
65.	Stanford Dingley	$5^1/_4$m	($8^1/_2$km)
66.	Hook Norton	$5^1/_4$m	($8^1/_2$km)
67.	Cropredy	$5^1/_4$m	($8^1/_2$km)
68.	Upper Lambourn	$5^1/_4$m	($8^1/_2$km)
69.	Deddington	$5^1/_4$m	($8^1/_2$km)
70.	Faringdon Folly	$5^1/_4$m	($8^1/_2$km)

71.	Sonning	$5^1/_4$m	($8^1/_2$km)
72.	Weston-on-the-Green	$5^1/_4$m	($8^1/_2$km)
73.	Shipton-Under-Wychwood	$5^1/_4$m	($8^1/_2$km)
74.	… and longer version	$7^1/_4$m	($11^1/_2$km)
75.	Cookham and Winter Hill	$5^1/_2$m	($8^3/_4$km)
76.	Stoke Talmage	$5^1/_2$m	($9^1/_2$km)
77.	Stanton St John	$5^1/_2$m	($8^3/_4$km)
78.	Hermitage	$5^1/_2$m	($8^3/_4$km)
79.	Hampstead Norreys	$5^1/_2$m	(9km)
80.	Burford	$5^1/_2$m	($8^3/_4$km)
81.	Hamstead Marshal	$5^1/_2$m	(9km)
82.	Middle Barton	$5^3/_4$m	($9^1/_4$km)
83.	Watlington Hill	6m	($9^1/_2$km)
84.	Walbury Hill and Coombe Gibbet	6m	($9^1/_2$km)
85.	Dorchester	6m	($9^1/_2$km)
86.	Uffington White Horse	6m	($9^1/_2$km)
87.	East Adderbury	6m	($9^1/_2$km)
88.	Enstone	6m	($9^1/_2$km)
89.	Barkham	6m	($9^1/_2$km)
90.	Abingdon	6m	($9^1/_2$km)
91.	… and longer version	$9^1/_2$m	($15^1/_4$km)
92.	Radcot Bridge	$6^1/_4$m	(10km)
93.	Great Coxwell	$6^1/_2$m	($10^1/_2$km)
94.	Waterperry and Waterstock	7m	(11km)
95.	North and South Stoke	7m	($11^1/_4$km)
96.	Charlbury	7m	(11km)
97.	… and longer version	$8^3/_4$m	(14km)
98.	Windsor Great Park	$7^1/_4$m	($11^1/_2$km)
99.	Thame	$7^1/_4$m	($11^1/_2$km)
100.	The Rollright Stones	$7^1/_2$m	(12km)

PUBLISHER'S NOTE

We very much hope that you enjoy the routes presented in this book, which has been compiled with the aim of allowing you to explore the area in the best possible way – on foot.

We strongly recommend that you take the relevant map for the area, and for this reason we list the appropriate Ordnance Survey maps for each route. Whilst the details and descriptions given for each walk were accurate at time of writing, the countryside is constantly changing, and a map will be essential if, for any reason, you are unable to follow the given route. It is good practice to carry a map and use it so that you are always aware of your exact location.

We cannot be held responsible if some of the details in the route descriptions are found to be inaccurate, but should be grateful if walkers would advise us of any major alterations. Please note that whenever you are walking in the countryside you are on somebody else's land, and we must stress that you should *always* keep to established rights of way, and *never* cross fences, hedges or other boundaries unless there is a clear crossing point.

Remember the country code:

Enjoy the country and respect its life and work
Guard against all risk of fire
Fasten all gates
Keep dogs under close control
Keep to public footpaths across all farmland
Use gates and stiles to cross field boundaries
Leave all livestock, machinery and crops alone
Take your litter home
Help to keep all water clean
Protect wildlife, plants and trees
Make no unnecessary noise

The walks are listed by length - from approximately 1 to 12 miles – but the amount of time taken will depend on the fitness of the walkers and the time spent exploring any points of interest along the way. Nearly all the walks are circular and most offer recommendations for refreshments.

Good walking.

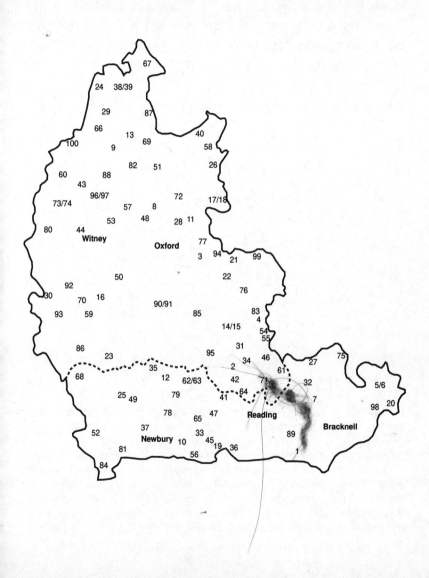

67

24 38/39

29

66

87

100 13 69 40

9 58

82 51 26

60 88

43

96/97 72

73/74 57 8 17/18

80 53 48 28 11

44 77

Witney **Oxford** 3 94 21 99

22

50 76

92 16

30 70 90/91 83

93 59 85 4

14/15 54
55

31

95 34 46 27 75

23 2 61

35 12 62/63 42 71 32 5/6

68 41 64 7 98 20

25 49 79

78 47 **Reading** 89 **Bracknell**

52 37 65

Newbury 10 33 1

45

81 56 19 36

84

Walk 1   FINCHAMPSTEAD RIDGES   3m (4³/₄km)

Maps: OS Sheets Landranger 175; Pathfinder 1189.

A walk through National Trust woodland and beside the River Blackwater, with a fairly steep climb up to the Ridges at the end.
Start: At 813635, the National Trust car park, Wellingtonia Avenue.

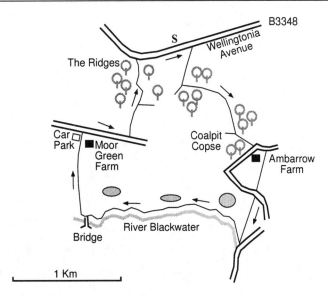

From the car park, walk down the entrance drive to the road (Wellingtonia Avenue) and turn left along the pavement for 100 yards. At Barn End, on the right, cross the road, with care, and follow the wide track, ascending gradually. At the top, just before the main track starts to descend steeply, turn left along a footpath into Fisher's Copse.

Keep to the main path as it meanders through the trees. At the far edge of the wood the path bends right and skirts the edge of a wood on the left, with a field on the right. At the field corner, near an iron gate, the path meets a cross-track: turn left and follow the track through Coalpit Copse (also known as Bluebell Wood) to reach a gate and road opposite Ambarrow Farm Cottage. Turn left along the road for 100 yards, passing Ambarrow Lodge on the left. When the road bends left, turn right down a footpath. Go through a gate and walk along the right edge of two fields to reach a minor road. Cross the road and go through the gate opposite.

Continue straight ahead, with a lake on your right, to pass a Windsurfing Club building and a car park on the left. Now keep to the main path as it swings right, then left, and go over a wooden bridge. Walk ahead on duckboards to reach a gate near a road. Do not go through the gate: instead, continue ahead along the path to reach a wide track beside the River Blackwater.

Turn right and follow the track for about a mile, keeping the River Blackwater on your left and **Moor Green Conservation area** on your right, until you reach a wooden bridge over the river. Just beyond the bridge, keep to the track on the right and follow it as it bends right, away from the river. The track brings you to a small car park: go through and out to the road.

Turn right for 200 yards, passing Moor Green Farm on the right, and then turn left up a wide track between houses. When the track bends right, continue ahead through a gap into the trees. Now with Spout Pond on your left, follow the path as it bends left, then right, uphill, to reach the once open spaces of **Finchampstead Ridges**. Continue to reach the road (Wellingtonia Avenue) and turn right for 100 yards before crossing the road, with care, to return to the car park.

POINTS OF INTEREST:

Moor Green Conservation Area – This is a nature area managed by the Berkshire, Buckinghamshire and Oxfordshire Naturalist Trust (BBONT). The three lakes you pass are filled gravel pits. A good variety of birds and plants can be seen. The River Blackwater also provides some interesting river-side plants.

Finchampstead Ridges – The Ridges are owned by the National Trust. Centuries ago the area was part of the great Windsor Forest. When that forest diminished in size it was found that the soil at the top of the ridges was unsuitable for agriculture and thus the area retained its woodland. In between the trees you may get some good views over the Blackwater Valley. Wellingtonia Avenue was constructed, in 1863, by the then MP, John Walters. The Wellingtonia trees, which can grow to over 300 ft, were planted in 1869.

REFRESHMENTS:

None on the route, but available in Crowthorne, just a short distance to the east.

Maps: OS Sheets Landranger 175; Explorer 3.
*A pleasant walk through the South Chiltern woods and a visit to
the 'Maharajah's Well'.*
Start: At 667831, the Four Horseshoes Inn, Checkendon.

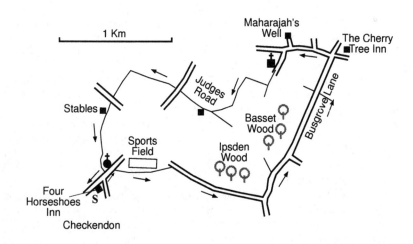

If you use the inn car park, please check with the landlord beforehand. Leave the inn
car park via its main road entrance and turn right along the road for 200 yards. Just
past the **church**, on your left, turn right along a track, signposted to the 'Pig Breeders
Co Workshops'. After 25 yards, bear left and go over a stile. There is a playing field
on the left. Continue ahead through a small wood and, still bearing left, go over a
cross-tracks. Now go through a gap in a hedge to reach a barn. Go to the left of the
barn and then diagonally across a field to a stile (on to a road) on the far side. Turn
right along the road and follow it downhill, through woodland, to reach a T-junction
in the valley bottom (Splashall Bottom). Turn left and follow a road which ascends
gradually up through Ipsden and Basset Woods. As you reach the top of the rise you
will have Busgrove Wood on your right. Continue along the road, which now descends
gradually to reach a crossroads at Stoke Row. The Cherry Tree Inn is to the right here.

Turn left and, when convenient, cross to the pavement on the other side. Continue for 300 yards, passing the Post Office and the Village Hall on the left, to arrive at **The Maharajah's Well** and a small park on the right. Continue along the road for another 100 yards to reach the church. Here, turn left along School Lane. When the houses on the right end, continue along a lane for approximately 150 yards to reach the end of first field on the right. Now, turn right along an enclosed path between fields (signposted for Checkendon). At the far side of the fields the path bends left, then right into Ipsden Wood. After 20 yards, turn left alongside an enclosure fence on the left and, when the enclosure ends, go straight on along the path, which bends right towards a wire fence on the right. The path now descends to meet a cross-tracks (Judges Road). Turn right, passing a house on the left, and follow the track to a road. Cross the road, with care, and go over the stile opposite. Head up the left edge of the field beyond, with a wood on your left, to reach the top left corner. Here, turn left and go through a gate into another field. Bear slightly right cross this field, aiming for the distant house on the right, to reach a stile. Go over and follow an enclosed path to reach a road.

Cross the road and take a path just to the right of a garage. Go through a gate into a stable yard and go ahead over a stile and across a paddock to reach another stile. Go over and turn left, then right, around the side of a second paddock. Go past a pond, on the left, and continue along a wide track for 200 yards to reach a six-barred gate on the right. Now veer left across another wide track to reach a gate and stile. Cross the stile and maintain direction to go diagonally across the field to reach a stile in the opposite corner. Cross and turn left along a path, following it to **Checkendon Church** and the drive to **Checkendon Court**. Turn left along the drive to reach a road and turn right for 200 yards to return to the start.

POINTS OF INTEREST:
Maharajah's Well – The well is 365 ft deep (approximately twice the height of Nelson's Column in Trafalgar Square). The money to build the well was given by the Maharajah of Benares to Mr A E Reade in 1863, as a token of friendship.
The Church of St Peter and St Paul, Checkendon – There are two Norman arches in the chancel and some 13th or 14th century fresco paintings on the walls of the apse.
Checkendon Court – The estate surrounding the Court dates back to around 1030.

REFRESHMENTS:
The Four Horseshoes Inn, Checkendon.
The Cherry Tree, Stoke Row.

Walk 3   **SHOTOVER PARK**   3¹/₄m (5¹/₄km)

Maps: OS Sheets Landranger 164; Pathfinder 1116.

A walk, with plenty of interest, from the village of Wheatley, through Shotover Park and back. The walk has one gradual climb.

Start: At 597057, St Mary the Virgin Church, Wheatley.

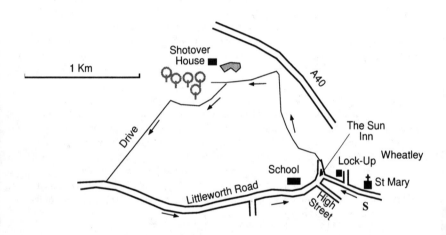

With your back to the church, turn right along Church Road to reach a crossroads. Cross, with care, and continue ahead. On the right you will pass an old, triangular-shaped **Lock-up**. Just before you reach the Sun Inn, bear right along Westfield Road. At the next crossroads, cross, with care, and continue along the road opposite to reach a stile near a gate. Go over and cross the field beyond to reach another stile in the far fence.

Go over and bear right across the field beyond to reach a stile in its far corner. The A40 is close by on the right. Cross the stile and turn left. Now ignore a track bearing off to the left, continuing ahead along a fenced drive. On the right there is an ornamental pond and, ahead and slightly to the right, you can see **Shotover House**.

On reaching a track junction, bear left. The track, level at first, soon starts to ascend: ignore all turnings to both right and left, continuing ahead, with woodland on your right. Where the wood bears away to the right, turn left along a wide avenue and follow it to reach a lane. Turn left along the lane, following it back towards Wheatley. Just after passing a school on the left, bear left along Littleworth Road. Continue past the High Street, on the right, and take the next turning on the right (Church Street).

Follow the road back to **St Mary the Virgin Church**, passing the Sun Inn, on the left.

POINTS OF INTEREST:
Wheatley Village Lock-up – Built in 1834, the pyramid-shaped lock-up has a floor which is approximately 6 foot square and headroom of about 8 foot. During the 19th century it was used to lock-up the drunk and disorderly before sending them to the court at Oxford.
Shotover House and Park – The first house on the site was built during the mid-17th century by Sir Timothy Tyrrell, who was Ranger of Shotover Forest at that time. The park is a designated area of outstanding beauty.
St Mary the Virgin Church – The church was designed by the Victorian architect George Edmund Street. It was consecrated in 1857.

REFRESHMENTS:
The Sun Inn, Wheatley. Being on the old coaching road, this old inn would almost certainly have been frequented by highwaymen.

Maps: OS Sheets Landranger 175; Explorer 3.

*A woodland walk, passing through an area of land once granted
by King Offa. There are a few gradual ascents and descents.*
Start: At 714931, the Fox and Hounds Inn, Christmas Common.

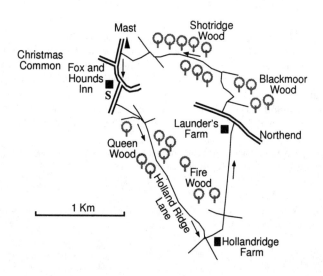

Parking is possible close to the inn. Now, with your back to the inn, cross the road, with care, and turn right. After 200 yards, at the far end of a row of Forestry Commission houses, turn left along the Oxfordshire Way. The church of the Nativity will be on your right. Go over at a cross-tracks, continuing ahead to reach a T-junction of tracks near a house. Turn left for 30 yards to reach Hollandridge Lane. Turn right and follow the lane through Queen Wood, towards **Hollandridge Farm**. Where the track bends left, just before the farm, turn left and walk along the right edge of a field. There is a pond on the right and, just beyond, are the farm buildings.

At the hedge corner, continue straight on across the middle of the field. Go over a stile on the far side and on down through a wood (curiously named Fire Wood). In the **valley bottom**, go straight over at a cross-tracks, following a bridleway uphill. On emerging from the wood, go through a gate and continue up a clearly defined path across a field. This path defines the boundary between Oxfordshire and Buckinghamshire.

Follow the path to Launder's Farm. Go through a gate and walk with the farm on your left. After 100 yards, where the track bends left, turn right through a gate. Follow the path beyond to a path junction and fork left to reach a road. Turn left along the road, looking out for a small stone pillar, marking the county boundary, on the left. After passing the last house on the right, turn right along a wide track, signed for Woodside. At the track end, continue ahead between fences. Go over a stile and across a narrow meadow, then over a second stile and into Shotridge Wood.

Bear left, following the direction of the white arrow waymarkers on the trees. The path bears right, then meanders, fairly steeply, downhill to reach a crossing path. Turn left. The path, level at first, soon starts to ascend the hillside. Deer can quite often be seen in this wood. The path starts to widen near the top: at a footpath junction, bear left, just inside the edge of the wood. Soon you join a wider track coming in from the right: bear left along this wider track.

At the next path junction, take the left fork to reach a broad track. Turn right, passing the radio mast, which is such a prominent feature of **Christmas Common,** on the right, to reach a road. Turn left and follow the road back to the Fox and Hounds Inn.

POINTS OF INTEREST:
Hollandridge Farm – The farm has records dating back to at least 1282.
The Valley Bottom in Fire Wood – The path you cross (part of the Oxfordshire Way) follows the route of a 774 AD boundary charter. Much of the land in this area would have been granted by King Offa.
Christmas Common – The area is said to be so named because at Christmas 1643, the Parliamentarians, who held Watlington, and the Royalists, who were defending the ridge, decided to call a temporary truce so that both armies could enjoy the local festivities.

REFRESHMENTS:
The Fox and Hounds Inn, Christmas Common.
There are also possibilities in Watlington.

Walks 5 & 6   **ETON**   3¹/₂m (5¹/₂km)
or 5m (8km)

Maps: OS Sheets Landranger 175; Pathfinder 1173.
A flat walk which includes the playing fields of Eton, part of the Thames towpath and good views of Windsor Castle.
Start: At 964774, Eton Court car park, just off Eton High Street.

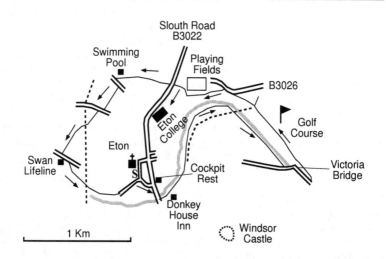

With your back to the meadows, leave the car park and go left, then right along Eton Court to reach the High Street. Cross the road and turn right towards the river. On the left you will pass **The Cockpit Restaurant**, with some old stocks just outside. Cross the river bridge and immediately turn left, down some steps, to the riverside road. Continue straight ahead to reach the Donkey House Inn, on the right. Keeping to the riverside, go along a fenced path (Romney Walk) to reach a lane. Turn left and, with the railway on your right, follow the lane to a boatyard. Go ahead through the yard and over a stile. Continue beside the River Thames for ³/₄ mile, passing under a railway bridge, to reach the B470 (Windsor Road) at Victoria Bridge. Turn left over the bridge and, after 200 yards, turn sharp left along a gravel track on to Datchet Golf Course. Turn left and keep to the left edge of the course to reach the far corner. Here, go ahead along a narrow path, with a wire fence on your right, then, at a footpath sign, turn left

16

through the railway arch (mind your head). At the far side, go through a wooden swing gate and bear left across three fields, crossing a stone bridge and two stiles before crossing a third stile just to the left of a boat-house. Cross a concrete slipway and go ahead along a drive to reach the B3026. Turn left for 75 yards, then turn left over a bridge into **Eton Playing Fields**. Follow the path ahead to reach a second bridge. Here, turn sharp right and follow the track which bends left to reach Slough Road.

The shorter walk turns left along the road, passing **Eton College**. Go ahead at the traffic lights and along Eton High Street. Go past Tangier Lane, on the left, then take the next right turn into Eton Court, and walk back to the car park.

The longer walk crosses the road, with care, and goes through the gate opposite. Go straight across a playing field and over a wooden bridge, then maintain direction on a track along the left edge of a second playing field. At Swimming Pool Cottages, bear left to reach a lane. Turn left for 50 yards, then go right over a stile. Bear left across the field beyond to go through a gate in the corner, near a red-brick building. Go along the left edge of a field to reach the B3026. Cross, with care, and bear right towards some allotments. At a metalled track, turn left and then, at the second footpath sign (look for the blue arrow) turn right under the railway. On the far side, bear left along a bridleway to reach Meadow Lane. Turn left past the *Swan Lifeline*, an organisation which looks after injured swans, mostly from the river Thames. Now, when the fence on the right ends, turn right, through a gap, into a field. Keeping the hedge on your right, head towards a bridge and the river. Turn left along the tow-path, going under the bridge, and heading back towards Eton. On reaching an open meadow (The Brocas), bear left across the field to return to the car park.

POINTS OF INTEREST:

The Cockpit Restaurant, Eton – Dating back to 1420, its name originates from the fact that the building at the rear was used for cock-fights during the 17th and 18th centuries.

Eton College and Playing Fields – Founded in 1440 by Henry VI, the college has a long and varied history. It is renowned for its past, and present, pupils. Against the wall between the playing fields and Slough Road the famous Eton Wall Game is played, on November 30th each year. Outside the main entrance is an 1864 iron street lamp known as the Burning Bush. The Library is a copy of the Radcliffe Camera in Oxford.

REFRESHMENTS:

There are numerous places in Eton, including those mentioned in the text.

17

Walk 7   **WALTHAM ST LAWRENCE**   3¹/₂m (5¹/₂km)
Maps: OS Sheets Landranger 175; Pathfinder 1173.
A level walk through farmland south of the village and returning
through Shottesbrooke Park. It can be muddy in places during
wet weather.
Start: At 829769, Waltham St Lawrence Church.

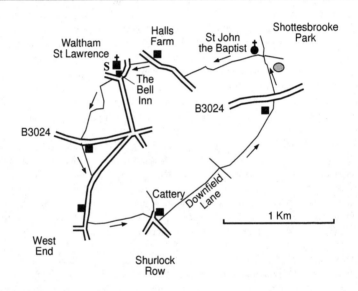

With your back to the church, go to the right of the enclosed triangle, then turn right
along the road. Almost immediately turn left into **Neville Close**. At the end of the
road, turn left and go across the middle of a field, heading for a point on the far
boundary, just to the right of a shed. Turn right, then left along the field edge, keeping
the hedge on your left, to reach a small footbridge and stile. Cross and bear slightly
right (not diagonally right) across the next field to reach a stile, and footbridge on to
a road (the B3024). Cross, with care, turn left for 10 yards, then turn right over a stile.
Cross the middle of the field beyond to reach a stile and footbridge. Cross on to a
road. Cross the road, with care, and turn right, noting the gallows at the entrance to
West End House on the right, as you pass. Just before reaching Sill Bridge, turn left

over a stile and cross a small field. Go through a gap in the hedge and continue across the middle of three fields to reach a stile in the far boundary of the third. Go over and follow a path between the rear of some houses, on the left, and a small stream, on the right, to reach Crockford's Bridge. Cross to the second road to reach Shurlock Row Boarding Cattery.

Turn right along the road, but, after 30 yards, turn left along a hedged bridleway (Downfield Lane). Follow this track for $^3/_4$ mile, then, when it bends sharply left, go straight on, crossing a stile and the middle of the field beyond to reach a gateway. Go through and walk ahead along a grass track, passing a cottage on the left. Here, the track becomes gravelled: continue along it to reach a road (the B3024). Cross, with care. Turn right for 10 yards, then turn left along a bridleway into Shottesbrook Park. Keeping the fence to your left, continue ahead to reach the **Church of St John the Baptist**. Here, turn left through a swing gate into the churchyard. Keep to the left of the church to go through an arch and continue along a walled path. Go through a second arch, then walk ahead to cross a stile.

Follow the field edge, with an 'ha ha' (a fence at the bottom of a ditch) on the right, then cross a stile next to a wooden gate. Continue ahead, with Burringham Wood on your left. Now go through some trees to reach a stile on to a road. Turn right along the road and, immediately after passing Halls Farm, on the right, turn left along a short gravel track. At the entrance to a cemetery, turn right along an enclosed path to reach a road. Turn left to return to the **Parish Church**.

POINTS OF INTEREST:

Neville Close, Waltham St Lawrence – The road is named after a local family who became lords of the manor in 1608. During the Civil War the family was divided between the Royalists and the Parliamentarians, an example of 'By the Sword divided'.

St John The Baptist Church, Shottesbrooke – The church is thought to be a scaled down model of Salisbury Cathedral. It was completed in 1337. One story states that a local smith climbed to the top of the spire to fix a weathervane. Unfortunately he was rather fond of drink and while on top lost his balance. He fell to his death and was buried on the spot.

Waltham St Lawrence Parish Church – The church dates back to the 11th century and is mentioned in the Doomsday Book. The yew tree in the churchyard is over 300 years old.

REFRESHMENTS:

The Bell, Waltham St Lawrence, a fine 14th century inn.

Walk 8   **THRUPP** $3^{1}/_{2}$m ($5^{1}/_{2}$ km)

Maps: OS Sheets Landranger 164; Pathfinder 1092.

A level walk alongside the Oxford Canal, across fields, and back alongside the River Cherwell.

Start: At 481158, the Boat Inn, Thrupp. Please park discreetly in the road nearby.

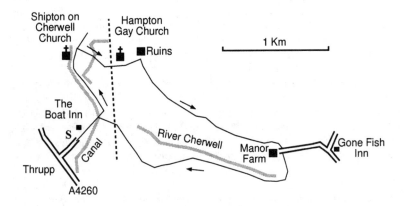

Facing the inn, turn right to reach the canal and turn left along the tow-path. Turn right over a canal bridge, then immediately go left to follow the tow-path again. Follow the tow-path as it bends left, around Thrupp Wide: as you continue you will have the canal on your left and the River Cherwell on your right. After 700 yards you will pass **Shipton on Cherwell Church** on the opposite bank. About 100 yards further on, you will reach a bridge over the canal: bear right, away from the canal, and turn right along a track.

After 30 yards, ignore a stile, on the left, but go over the one directly ahead. Bear left across the field beyond to cross a bridge over the River Cherwell. Veer right across the next field, keeping to the right of a tree. Aim to the right of Hampton Gay Church, which you can see ahead of you, to reach a **railway line**. Cross, with care, into the field on the other side. St Giles' Church is now on the left.

Head across the field, aiming towards the corner of a fence just to the right of the ruins of Hampton Gay Manor. Here, turn right across the field, heading towards the distant steeple of Hampton Poyle Church. At the far side of the field, continue ahead, with a fence on your right, to reach the far corner. Cross a stile and go across the next field, bearing slightly right to follow the direction of the waymarker arrow.

Cross a stile and walk ahead across the middle of the field beyond to reach a bridge. Cross the bridge and the next field to reach another bridge and a stile. Cross these and continue ahead, aiming for the left side of Manor Farm. Cross a stile in a wooden fence and bear right to reach a gate in the corner of a small field. Go through and bear left across a field, keeping to the left of the farm and a small church. Cross two stiles in the left-hand field boundary, and turn right for 20 yards to cross another two stiles.

Continue across a field to reach a lane, just to the left of the church. Cross the lane and go over the stile opposite. Now head across a field to reach a stile near the corner of a garden. Go over and bear right to reach a small bridge. Cross and bear right again along a field edge, then cross a bridge over the River Cherwell. At the far side, turn right and follow the river bank, with the river on your right.

At a field corner, go through a gate and continue ahead. Just before the next field corner the path veers left, away from the river, to go through a gap in the hedge. Cross the middle of the next field to reach the river bank again, continuing ahead to reach, and pass under, the railway line. Now go along a track and then through the British Waterways yard to reach the canal. Go over the canal bridge and turn left to retrace your steps back to **Thrupp** and the Boat Inn.

POINTS OF INTEREST:

Shipton on Cherwell Church – This church was once known as the bargee's church, due to the number of canal users attending the services.

Railway Line – Near this spot was the site of one of the first railway disasters in the country, in 1874 when 30 passengers were killed in a derailment. Queen Victoria sent a telegram of sympathy to the local people.

Thrupp – The canal, and the inn, have been featured in an episode from the Inspector Morse series.

REFRESHMENTS:

The Boat Inn, Thrupp.

The Gone Fish Inn, Hampton Poyle.

Walk 9   **GREAT TEW** $3^{1}/_{2}$m ($5^{1}/_{2}$km)

Maps: OS Sheets Landranger 164; Pathfinder 1068.

This undulating walk crosses agricultural land to the south and south-east of one of the most picturesque villages in Oxfordshire.

Start: At 394293, Great Tew car park.

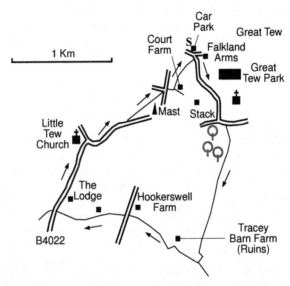

Leave the car park through the main entrance and turn left. Almost immediately, fork right up a road signed for St Michael's Church. As you walk up the road you should be able to see parts of Great Tew Park on your left. Continue past the arched entrance to the church, on the left, to reach a road junction with a small grass triangle. Take the left fork and, after 20 yards, bear left across the road to reach the track/drive opposite.

When you reach the house, on the left, go ahead through a gate and along the edge of a field, walking with a small wood on your right. At the far field corner, do not veer right into the copse: instead, carry straight on along the right edge of the next two fields. At the far corner of the second field, with a small copse on your right, go over a stile and, after 5 yards, turn right along a narrow path through trees. Now go along the left edge of a field.

At the far side, go through a gate. The ruins of Tracey Barn Farm are on the right. Bear left to reach a second gate. Go through and turn right along the field edge, walking with a hedge and a small stream on the right. Follow the farm track along the edge of three fields to reach a road (the B4022). Hookerswell Farm is just to your right here. Cross the road, with care, and continue along the track opposite. The small stream is still on your right. Where the track turns right, to reach a house on the other side of the stream, continue ahead along the field edge.

At the far side of the field, go through a gate, and continue along the edge of the next field. At the far corner, go through a gap on to a road. Turn right, following the road past 'The Lodge', on the right, to reach a T-junction at Little Tew. The **Church of St John The Evangelist** is on your left. Turn right along Great Tew Road. After 400 yards, just beyond the top of the hill, look for a footpath on the left signed 'Great Tew $\frac{1}{2}$'. Turn left through the gap in the hedge, then bear diagonally right across a field, aiming well left of a radio mast.

Go over a stile at the far side, and cross the road beyond to reach the footpath opposite. Cross a stile by a double gate, and follow a fence and trees, on the left, bearing left down a field towards Court Farm. Go through a gate, pass to the left of the silos, and turn right. After 10 yards, turn left over a stile and go diagonally right down a field, keeping about 20 yards to the right of two large trees, to reach a swing gate in the right-hand hedge. Go through and turn left down a road towards a telephone kiosk. The entrance to the car park in **Great Tew** is just to the left of the kiosk.

POINTS OF INTEREST:
The Church of St John The Evangelist, Little Tew – The main attraction of this village church is its unusual saddleback tower built in 1835 by George Street.
Great Tew – This very attractive village is well worth looking around. Many of the cottages were, from 1819, built or embellished in traditional style for Matthew Boulton, the son of a steam engine manufacturer. Each cottage is unique in some way. The popular 15th-century inn, the Falkland Arms, is also well worth a visit. It is named after Lucius Cary, the 17th-century Lord Falkland, who entertained many notable guests at Great Tew Park.

REFRESHMENTS:
The Falkland Arms, Great Tew.

Walk 10 **WOOLHAMPTON** 3³/₄m (6km)

Maps: OS Sheets Landranger 174; Pathfinder 1187.

A walk through Midgham Park and along part of the Kennet Canal. Can be muddy in parts during wet weather.

Start: At 573666, the Midgham Station car park, Woolhampton.

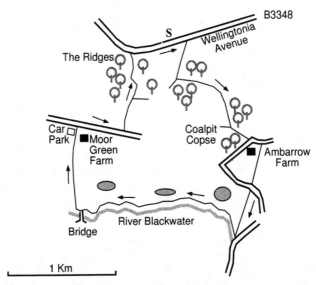

From the car park entrance of Midgham Station, turn left along Station Road to reach the A4. Note the **Fountain** on the corner. Turn left for 200 yards, passing a craft shop along the way. Now cross the road, with care, and go up New Road Hill opposite. Near the top you will pass the entrance to Hall Court Farm, on the left. Continue along the road for another 100 yards to reach the East Lodge of Midgham Park, where the road bends right. Here, turn left over stile and follow a well-defined path through Midgham Park. Cross over two further stiles as the path descends gradually to reach a gate. Over to your right you should be able to see the clock tower, and the top, of **Midgham House**. Go through the gate and bear right across the meadow beyond to reach another gate and a gravel drive.

Cross the drive and go through the gate opposite. Now follow a wide track. The track is level at first, but soon starts to ascend gradually towards Midgham Church, the spire of which can be seen on the hilltop. Go through a gate and up through an avenue of trees, and a hollow, to reach West Lodge, and, just beyond, a road. The entrance to Midgham Church, and a wooden seat, are on the left.

Continue down the road (Church Road) to reach the A4. The Coach and Horses Inn is just on the right. Cross the A4, with care, and go along the short drive opposite to reach a stile. Go over and cross the middle of the small field beyond to reach a stile at the far side. Cross on to a road and walk ahead along it, crossing a railway bridge and then a canal bridge. Immediately after crossing the canal bridge, go through a gate on the right. Go down a slope and, at the bottom, turn sharp right to go under the road bridge, keeping the canal on your left.

The route now follows the tow-path back to Woolhampton. It crosses the canal twice, first at Cranwell Bridge and then at Oxlease Bridge. Continue past Woolhampton Lock to reach a road. The **Row Barge Inn** is on your right here. Turn left over the canal bridge and then go over the railway crossing. Now turn left back into the Station car park.

POINTS OF INTEREST:
The Fountain, Woolhampton – The, now dry, fountain was erected in 1897 to commemorate the Diamond Jubilee of Queen Victoria.
Midgham House – The manor house dates back to the 13th century. For over 400 years it remained in the hands of the Erley Family. It was sold to Stephen Poyntz in 1738. Poyntz became a tutor of William, Duke of Cumberland, the son of George II.
The Row Barge Inn, Woolhampton – The current building is over 400 years old. It is said that King Edward VII used to call at the inn after visiting Newbury races.

REFRESHMENTS:
The Angel Inn, Woolhampton.
The Falmouth Arms, Woolhampton.
The Coach and Horses, on the A4 at Midgham.
The Row Barge Inn, Woolhampton.

Walk 11   **NOKE AND ODDINGTON**   3³/₄m (6km)

Maps: OS Sheets Landranger 164; Pathfinder 1092.

An easy walk across part of Otmoor, passing through the interesting village of Oddington, where a Maori Princess is buried in the churchyard.

Start: At 544132, the Parish Church of St Giles, Noke.

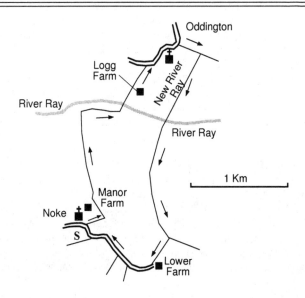

Facing St Giles' Church, take the road to the right, and, where the road bends right, go straight ahead along a bridleway, walking between the churchyard and a house. At a T-junction, turn left along a path signed 'Oddington 1½'. Walk past an entrance to Manor Farm, on the left, and after a further 30 yards, turn right along a track, walking with a hedge on the left and a ditch on the right. Soon there are hedges left and right.

On reaching a large stone agricultural tank on the right, continue ahead along the field edge, keeping to the left of a ditch and hedge, to reach the River Ray. Here, turn right for 400 yards, then turn left and cross two bridges over the old and new River Ray. At the far side, go ahead across a field to reach a track. Turn right towards Logg Farm.

After 70 yards, turn left along an indistinct path, keeping just to the left of two large barns. When you reach the farm drive, turn left along an avenue of trees to reach a road. Turn right and follow the road to reach **St Andrew's Church, Oddington**, on the right. Continue on along the road, noting, where it bends right, the **Victorian Letter Box** set in the building wall on the left.

Follow the road around to the right, then, when the road bends left, carry straight on along a track which starts just to the right of a telephone box. Follow the track to reach a bridge over the River Ray. Cross and turn right along a broad track. Continue over the old River Ray. Where the gravelled track turns left into a field, continue straight on along a grassy track.

Go through a metal gate and continue ahead, walking with a ditch on your right. In the distance you can see the Beckley radio mast on the hill top. On reaching a stone bridge on the right, near a telegraph pole, turn right over the bridge and walk ahead along a track. Pass Lower Farm on your left, continuing to reach a lane. Turn right and follow the lane, which bends left near some thatched cottages, back to St Giles' Church.

POINTS OF INTEREST:

St Andrew's Church, Oddington – Buried in the churchyard is Margaret Staple Brown, nee Papakura, a Maori Princess who died on the 19th April 1930. Her grave is near the entrance to the church. Visitors from New Zealand often pay their respects as you can see from the visitors' book.

Oddington – The village is said to have two medicinal wells, whose waters were claimed to cure Moor Evil, which affected cattle. The author, John Buchan, writes about it in his novel *Midwinter*.

REFRESHMENTS:

The inn marked on the OS map in Noke village is now closed, so there are no refreshments on the route. The nearest refreshments are in Islip, a little to the west.

Walk 12   **EAST ILSLEY** $3^3/_4$m (6km)

Maps: OS Sheets Landranger 174; Pathfinder 1155.

Starting from a once well-known sheep market village, this walk gently ascends the Berkshire Downs, from where there are fine views over the South Oxfordshire plain.

Start: At 493812, the Crown and Horns Inn, East Ilsley.

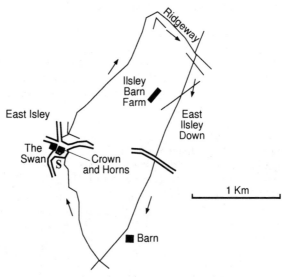

If you use the inn car park, please check with the landlord beforehand. From the inn, cross the road, with care, and go down the 'No Through Road' opposite. After 200 yards, just opposite the last barn on the left, turn right along a track, between houses. Follow the track for 100 yards to reach a path junction. Here, turn left up a bridleway, walking between paddocks, on the right, and a field, on the left. At the end of the paddocks the track continues along the left edge of a large field. On the hillside to the right you can see Ilsley Barn Farm. Continue along the well-defined track, gently ascending the Downs. This walk, although it ascends the Berkshire Downs, contrasts interestingly with the West Ilsley walk. The prominent feature here is farmland, whereas the dominant features on the western village walk are the many racehorse gallops.

At the top of the Downs, go over a racehorse gallop and continue for a further 10 yards to reach a wide crossing track (the Ridgeway). Turn right and follow the Ridgeway, looking to the left for some excellent views across the South Oxfordshire Plain. The cooling towers of Didcot Power Station stand out in the distance. Just before you reach the concrete drive leading to Ilsley Barn Farm, there is a water tap, on the right, providing drinking water for thirsty walkers. Below it is a small trough for our four-legged friends. Continue along the Ridgeway for another 300 yards to reach a cross-tracks. Here, turn right along a byway, walking between fences. At the next cross-tracks, go straight over, passing to the left of a copse. Stay on the main track as it descends to reach a road. Cross the road, with care, and continue along the track opposite. The track gradually ascends the hillside with, over to your right, a view of East Ilsley. Ignore a track leading off to the right, continuing ahead, uphill, to pass to the right of some barns.

At the next cross-tracks, just before an orange signpost stating that there is no route for horses across the A34, turn right down a track. The A34 can be seen to your left. Follow the track as it descends, and then ascends towards East Ilsley. As it nears the village it bends left, then right, passing a sports field on the right. Go through a gate/gap and along the road beyond, passing a school, and then the village church, on the left. The road bends left, then right, as it descends towards the centre of the village. On reaching a road junction, continue ahead to pass the village pond on the right. At the next road junction, turn left and follow the road back to the Crown and Horns Inn, on the left.

If you continue past the inn and turn left along the road which runs between the it and the Swan Inn, then, after about 150 yards, on the left, you will reach two interesting sites. The first is an old milestone dated 1776. The second, just a few yards further on, is a plaque about the **East Ilsley** sheep fairs.

POINTS OF INTEREST:

East Ilsley – Due to its close proximity to the Ridgeway, East Ilsley, or Market Ilsley as it was once called, became a centre for sheep fairs. So busy was its trade that only London's Smithfield Market was larger. The fairs are thought to date back to medieval times. The plaque, visited on the short extension to the walk, reveals that the last Fair was held in 1934. A tape about the fairs is held in Reading Museum.

REFRESHMENTS:
The Crown and Horns Inn, East Ilsley.
The Swan Inn, East Ilsley.

Walk 13   **BARFORD ST MICHAEL** $3^3/_4$m (6km)
Maps: OS Sheets Landranger 151; Pathfinder 1045.
An undulating walk taking you close to the site of Ilbury Iron Age Fort. The views from the hill should compensate for some road walking during the latter stages.
Start: At 432326, Barford St Michael Church.

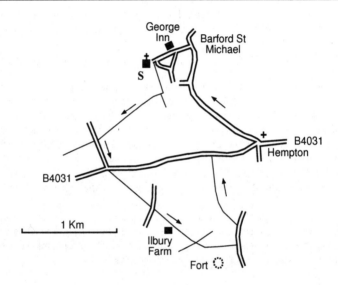

Go through the upper church gates and immediately turn left along the left edge of the churchyard, following it to reach a stile in the corner. Cross and go along the edge of the field beyond. Cross another stile, and a footbridge, in the far corner and turn right along the edge of the next field. At a hedge corner, bear diagonally left across the field to reach a gate in the hedge. Go through, and maintain direction, across the next field - which may be ploughed - to reach a stile at the far left-hand corner. Go over on to a road.

Turn left along the road to reach a T-junction with the B4031. Cross, with care, and go through the gate opposite. Bear left along a broad track across a field, and then go along the right-hand edge of a second field to reach a road. Cross and continue along the road to Ilbury Farm, opposite. Go through the farmyard and a gate at the far side and continue ahead along a track across fields. Over to your right is the mound of **Ilbury Iron Age Fort**. Go over a crossing path, and continue ahead to reach the field corner.

Go through a gap and bear left along the field edge, keeping a hedge to your left, to reach a road at the far end. Turn left, then, after 150 yards, turn left again through a gap in the field boundary, and bear right across the field. Go through a second gap and up the next field, going over a crossing path. At the far left-hand corner of the field, bear right to go along the left edge of the next field. At a hedge corner, on the left, bear right for 15 yards, then turn left up the right edge of a field. The hedge is now on your right: follow it to reach a road.

The path opposite is blocked here, so you must turn right along the road to reach the village of Hempton. At the first cross-roads, turn left along a road signed for Barford St Michael. As you walk down this road there are excellent views to your right. Ignore a road on the left, continuing ahead through the village. Go past a second junction and continue downhill. At the bottom of the hill, turn left along Lower Street. Go past the George Inn, on the right, and, after 400 yards, turn left up a road. The **church** is on the right.

POINTS OF INTEREST:
Ilbury Iron Age Fort – Berkshire and Oxfordshire have quite a varied selection of these forts scattered around the countryside. This one, another for your collection, is on private land and so can only be seen from the path.

Barford St Michael Church – This 12th-century church is said to contain some of the best Norman carvings in the country. In 1549, the vicar, James Webbe, earned the village national attention when he held a revolt against the government's insistence of the use of the English Prayer Book.

REFRESHMENTS:
The George Inn, Barford St Michael.

Walks 14 & 15   **EWELME**   3³/₄m (6km)
                                             or 6³/₄m (10³/₄km)

Maps: OS Sheets Landranger 175; Explorer 3.
An undulating walk in a beautiful part of the Oxfordshire countryside.
Start: At 647912, the Recreation Ground car park, Ewelme.

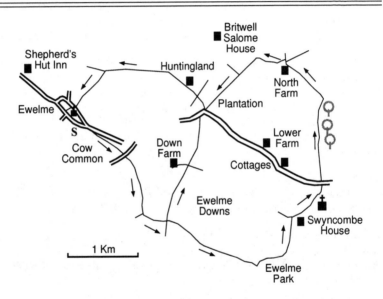

Facing the recreation ground, turn left through a swing gate and go along the left edge of a field (**Cow Common**). On reaching a stile on the left, do not cross but bear right across the corner of the field to reach a swing gate in the far hedge. Go through and cross the lane beyond to reach an enclosed track (Grindon Lane) opposite. Cross a farm track and continue along the gradually ascending track to reach a T-junction with a broad track. Turn left, downhill, to reach a track junction.

The shorter walk turns left here, going up the slope. Go past some piglet pens on the right to reach the farm road to Down Farm, on the left. Cross the road and continue up the left edge of a field, walking with a hedge on your left. At the far corner, continue along the right edge of the next field, now walking with a hedge on your right. On

32

reaching a road, turn right and, after 100 yards, at a sharp right-hand bend, continue ahead up a wide track for 30 yards, then turn left along a broad track, rejoining the longer walk.

The longer walk continues along the valley bottom. Ascending gently at first, the track narrows down to a path which goes up the right edge of a field, keeping to the left of a hedge. At the top corner, go through a gap and along an enclosed track, with Ewelme Park, on the right, and a copse on the left. Immediately after passing some stables on the left, turn left towards an open barn. At the barn, turn right along the Ridgeway. Follow the wide track, ascending gradually and going around a field edge to enter a wood (Jacob's Tent). The path descends steeply through the wood. On emerging, go through a swing gate and down a field to reach a second gate. Go through, and, after 15 yards, turn right along a tree-lined track. At a cross-tracks, with Swyncombe Church on the right, bear right and follow a lane, which bends left, to reach a road. Cross and go through the swing gate opposite. Go down, and up, the left edge of the field beyond, then up through trees to reach the top of the hill. From here the track descends fairly steeply, and bends left to reach North Farm. Here, bear right to reach a farm gate. Go through and, after 10 yards, at a broad crossing track, leave the Ridgeway, turning left along a track. Where the main track bends right, towards Britwell Salome House, carry on for another 800 yards, before turning right to rejoin the short walk.

Follow the right of way past a farm on the right, then, when the gravel track ends, continue along a grass track. Just before the track goes under an arch of trees, turn left over a stile. Bear diagonally right across the field beyond and, at the far side, go over a stile and along an enclosed path to reach a road, with **Ewelme Church and Almshouses** just opposite. Cross the road and turn right. After 20 yards, bear left down a path at the side of the churchyard to reach a road. Turn left, passing Ewelme Primary School, and, after a further 400 yards, turn right into the starting car park.

POINTS OF INTEREST:

Cow Common – During the Second World War the Common, taken over by the Government, was used to produce food. An auction for grazing rights is still held.
Ewelme Church and Almshouses– The church - which was built in 1436 - and the village were featured in the film version of John Mortimer's book *Paradise Postponed*. The almshouses were built in 1437. Once there were 13, but now there are only 8. From whichever direction they are approached there is a slight hill to climb.

REFRESHMENTS:
The Shepherd's Hut Inn, Ewelme.

Walk 16　　　**BUCKLAND AND PUSEY**　　　$3\frac{3}{4}$m (6km)

Maps: OS Sheets Landranger 164; Pathfinder 1135.

A fairly level walk across farmland, with a chance to view the two grand houses of Pusey and Buckland.

Start: At 344980, the Memorial Hall car park, Buckland.

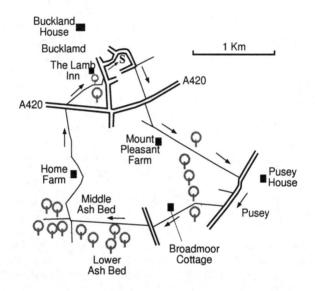

Leave the car park via the main entrance and turn right along the road. Where the road bends sharp right, continue straight ahead along a bridleway. On reaching the A420, cross, with care, and turn right. After 20 yards, turn left, go over two stiles, and along a track, walking with a hedge on the right. After 200 yards, before reaching Mount Pleasant Farm, bear left across a field, keeping just to the right of a line of telegraph posts. At the far side, cross two electric fences and continue in the same direction, still following the line of telegraph posts. There are good views to the right from here.

　　Cross a stile, go through scrub, and continue ahead along a farm track to reach a stile and road at the far side. This part of the route can be found on maps of the 18th and 19th centuries. The entrance to **Pusey House** is just opposite, but to get a good view of it, turn left, along the road, for 150 yards. Retrace your steps and continue along the road to reach a road junction. Here, fork right towards Gainfield. About 20 yards beyond a tall, tree-lined hedge, on the right, turn right along an enclosed bridleway signed 'Faringdon 4'.

Go through Gimbro Copse, through a gate, and then along the right edge of a field, walking with a wire fence on the right. Pass Broadmoor Cottage, on the right, continuing to reach a road. Cross and continue along the track opposite. Go through a belt of woodland (Middle Ash Bed) and continue ahead to reach a cross-tracks at the far end of a field on the right. Here, turn right. Now, when the woodland on the left ends, bear right, keeping to the main track.

Continue past a stone dovecote, on the right, and a house, Home Farm, on the left, staying on the main track as it bends left, and following it to reach the A420 again. Cross, with care, and go along the footpath opposite, going between two stone pillars, then passing the front of Croft Lodge. Go over a stile, and bear diagonally right across a field. Now, just before you reach a stile in the right-hand fence, look left for a good view of **Buckland House**.

Go over the stile and follow the path beyond through woodland to emerge at a road. Turn left and, after 200 yards, with the Lamb Inn slightly hidden on the left, turn right at a road junction. Follow the road through the attractive village of Buckland to reach another road junction. Here, bear right and, after 50 yards, by a telephone kiosk, turn right back into the Memorial Hall car park.

POINTS OF INTEREST:

Pusey House – It is thought that the original manor of Pusey was granted to William Pewse in 1015 by the Viking King Cnut (Canute). The present house was built in 1750. Edward Pusey was one of the leaders of the Oxford Movement which, during the 19th century, called for reform of the Church of England.

Buckland House – Built in 1757 for Sir Robert Throckmorton, the house was enlarged in 1910. The deer park behind the house dates back to the 13th century. It was redesigned by Capability Brown in 1760. In 1811 Sir John Throckmorton, a later member of the family that owned the house, made a bet that a coat could be made from wool sheared, spun, woven and dyed all in the same day. He won his bet. The coat can be seen in Newbury museum.

REFRESHMENTS:

The Lamb Inn, Buckland.

PIDDINGTON $3^3/_4$m (6km)
                                          or $5^1/_4$m ($8^1/_2$km)

Maps: OS Sheets Landranger 164; Pathfinder 1093.

A fairly hilly walk providing some excellent views from the top of Muswell Hill, and on the longer walk, from Brill.

Start: At 640169, St Nicholas' Church, Piddington.

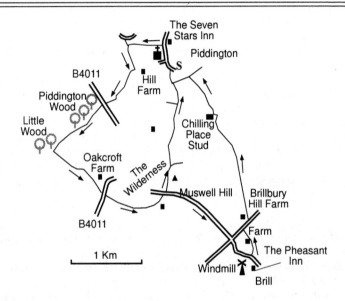

With the **church** on your left, go along the road for 200 yards. Just before the Seven Stars Inn, on the right, turn left over a stile. Cross the middle of the field beyond, go through a gate and across a second field. At the far side, turn left along the edge of three fields, passing Hill Farm, over to your left. At the far side of the third field, go through a gate and bear right across the field beyond. Go through a swing gate, turn right and, after 30 yards, turn left along the field edge to reach a road (the B4011). Cross, with care, go over the stile opposite and continue along an enclosed path just inside the edge of Piddington Wood. Go over a stile, then along the right edge of a field. At the far side, turn left along a farm track. Now, with a hedge on your right, follow the track towards Oakcroft Farm. When the track veers left, continue along the edge of three fields to reach the B4011 again. Cross diagonally right, with care, and go through a gate just to the left of the 'Bucks' county sign. Go up the left edge of a field, through a gate and continue, ascending quite steeply, along the right edge of the next field to reach a road at the top of Muswell Hill.

The shorter walk bears right across the road. Go along the gravelled drive opposite and, after 350 yards, just after a sharp right-hand bend, turn left through a gate. Now follow the yellow arrow waymarkers, keeping to the top right edge of an open area called The Wilderness. The path, level at first, soon starts to descend fairly steeply. Go over a broken stile, then along the edge of a small plantation. Cross a double stile and continue over two further stiles before bearing left down the next field to reach a stile in the bottom left-hand corner. The longer route is rejoined here.

The longer walk turns right along the road to reach a cross-roads. Go straight on up North Hill. At the top of the hill, on the right, is Brill Windmill, a weather-boarded postmill built in about 1680. When you are parallel with the windmill, turn left, passing the 'North Hill' sign. After 20 yards, turn left down a path, which soon becomes a track. At a junction, carry straight on, downhill, then, where the track bends right, go ahead through a kissing gate. Go past a building on the left, then follow a fence, also on the left, all the way around, passing a farmhouse, to reach a drive. Turn right down the drive to reach a road. Turn right and, after 150 yards, turn left over a stile. Now, with Brillbury Hall Farm on your left, bear right across four small paddocks. At the far side, continue across several fields, following the direction of yellow arrow waymarkers to reach Chilling Place Stud. Cross a drive and pass to the right of the farmhouse. After 150 yards, turn left through a swing-gate. Follow the fence on the left, around to reach a footbridge, cross, and bear left across two fields. At the far side of the second field, cross another footbridge, then immediately turn left along the field edge, walking with a hedge on your left. Cross the footbridge in the corner, then head along the right edge of the field beyond to reach a stile and the shorter route.

Go over the stile and turn right towards Piddington. Bear slightly left across the field, heading towards the houses. At the houses, go through a gate and turn left along a lane, following it back to Piddington Church.

POINTS OF INTEREST:
St Nicholas' Church, Piddington – Built about 1300, the church contains a mural of St Christopher. John Drinkwater, the playwright, is buried in the churchyard.

REFRESHMENTS:
The Seven Stars Inn, Piddington.
The Pheasant Inn, Brill.

Walk 19   UFTON COURT AND UFTON WOOD   4m (6¹/₂km)

Maps: OS Sheets Landranger 175; Pathfinder 1188.

A fairly level walk passing some medieval ponds and an Elizabethan, Tudor Style house.

Start: At 628650, the Round Oak Inn, Padworth Common.

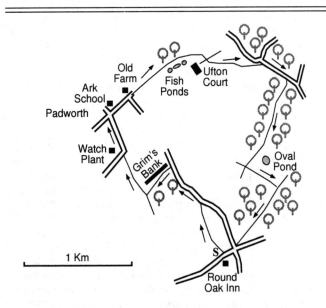

If you use the inn car park, please check with the landlord beforehand. From the front of the inn, cross the road, with care, and go along the footpath/drive opposite, keeping to the left. On reaching the house, on the right, continue ahead to reach a small enclosed area. Go through the iron gate ahead and along the right edge of the field beyond to reach a stile in the far corner. Cross the middle of the next field to a stile in a wire fence. Go over and bear left, aiming for a point about 25 yards short of the far left corner. Go over a stile and turn right along a narrow path, through trees, to reach Silver Lane. Turn left into a dip and climb the other side. At the top, just before a tall wire fence on the left, turn left along a footpath, heading through the trees. Over to your right you should be able to make out the feature of Grim's Bank, an ancient fortification which runs parallel to the path. At a T-junction, turn right and follow a path, with a high wire fence on the right, to reach a road. Turn right along the road, which bends sharply left, following it uphill to a crossroads. Turn right, passing the Ark School on the left. Situated as it is on the hill overlooking the Kennet and Avon Valley it is not too difficult to figure out why it was so named. Continue to the entrance of Old Farm. Now do not follow the road around to the right: instead, go through the farm gate (please close it) and head down an enclosed path, keeping a barn on your left.

At the bottom the path crosses a stone bridge, then ascends gradually through trees. As you ascend look to your right to see the **medieval fish ponds** in the grounds of Ufton Court. At the top of the incline, go through a metal barrier and turn right to reach the main drive of **Ufton Court**. Keep an eye open for a good view of the house. Cross the drive and continue ahead across a grassy area, aiming for a solitary, fenced evergreen tree which was presented by W R Benyon Esq. to mark the **Marvyn Dole** from 1581-1981.

At the tree, turn left to reach a signed stile in a hedge. Cross and bear right, crossing the field diagonally to the opposite corner. Here, turn left, past a barrier, to reach a road. Turn right and follow the road for 375 yards, then turn right, past a barrier, into Ufton Wood. Now ignore all turnings to the left and right, following the main track to reach the Oval Pond, on the left. Beyond the pond the path ascends a small rise and swings left to reach a crossing track (note the forestry notice on the left giving information about the wood – look out for more as you proceed). Turn left and walk to the next crossing track. Turn right along a wide track (with tall conifers on the left) to reach a barrier and road. Turn left for a few yards to reach a crossroads. Now turn right for 120 yards to return to the Round Oak Inn.

POINTS OF INTEREST:

Medieval Fish Ponds – This small group of ponds in the grounds of Ufton Court were once used to store fish. They are thought to date from medieval times.

Ufton Court – The Court is a Tudor style house built in 1576 during the reign of Elizabeth I. It once contained six hiding places and an escape tunnel for priests. Today it is used by the local Education Authority. It is not open to the public.

Marvyn Dole – Back in the 16th century the lady of the house got lost in the woods. She was found by local villagers. She was so pleased at being found that once a year she would issue the local people with bread and flour. The tradition still continues today with the issue of a blanket or duvet.

REFRESHMENTS:

The Round Oak, Padworth Common.

Walk 20   **WRAYSBURY**   4m (6$\frac{1}{2}$km)

Maps: OS Sheets Landranger 176; Pathfinder 1174.

A flat walk, partly alongside the Thames, overlooking the meadows where the Magna Carta was signed centuries ago.

Start: At 005742, the car park on the north side of The Green, Wraysbury.

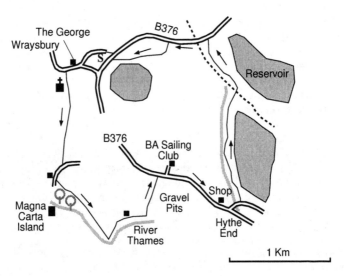

From the car park, turn left along the Green, passing a sports field on the left. At the T-junction, cross the road, with care, and turn right. After 150 yards, turn left into St Andrew's Close. Go through the church's lych gate and through the churchyard, keeping left of the **church**, to reach a metal gate. Go through and head across a field, keeping to the right of a large tree to reach a stile. Cross and follow the enclosed path beyond. Maintain direction over two stiles, then, when the enclosed path ends, cross the middle of the next field to reach a wooden bridge. Cross and go down the right edge of the next field to a stile on to a lane. Go ahead along the lane for 50 yards, passing a house on the right, then turn left along an enclosed footpath, following it around a small copse to reach the bank of the River Thames. Across the river are the meadows where, it is said, King John signed the **Magna Carta** in the 13th century.

Turn left, over a stile, and follow the path which runs alongside the River Thames. The river bends left and then right. Just before it bends right, over to your left you should see the remains of an old **Priory**. The ruins are on private property so keep to the river bank and continue ahead, eventually reaching a red brick wall. Turn left here, away from the river, following an enclosed path to the B376. The lakes on the right are water filled gravel pits. Cross the road, with care, and turn right, passing the entrance to the British Airways Sailing Club. After $^1/_2$ mile, at Hythe End, follow the road (Wraysbury Road) around a sharp left-hand bend. Cross a bridge and turn left at a footpath sign.

Go down steps and walk ahead through a gap in a hedge. The path now runs between the Colne Brook, on the left, and a large lake, on the right. This area provides an interesting variety of plants and birds. When the lake on the right ends, the path veers right to reach an area of open ground. Here, you should bear left, heading towards the high reservoir bank to reach a stile and railway crossing. Cross the railway, go over a stile, and turn left along an enclosed path which runs parallel with the railway. The path veers right and crosses a small bridge to reach a road: turn left, going over river and railway bridges, then immediately turn left, down some steps. At the bottom, turn right along the station approach road.

When the approach road joins the main road, continue along the pavement for 100 yards, then turn left into Tithe Road. Walk past Tithe Farm, on the left, and, when you reach a bungalow, keep to the right along an enclosed path which runs between a large lake on the left and houses on the right. The path emerges at a road opposite Wraysbury Baptist Church: cross the road and turn right. After 120 yards, at the Perseverance Inn, turn left down a road, and go over a wooden footbridge, noting the cottage on the left. After a further 40 yards, turn left to return to the starting car park.

POINTS OF INTEREST:
Parish Church of St Andrew, Wraysbury – There was a church on this site in Saxon times. The current building dates mainly from the 13th century. The font has been used to baptise the children of the village for over 700 years.
Magna Carta Island/Meadows – King John signed the Magna Carta here on the 15th June 1215.
Priory – The Priory was built in about 1160 to house Benedictine Nuns. Very little of it remains today.

REFRESHMENTS:
The George Inn, Wraysbury.
The Perseverance Inn, Wraysbury.

Walk 21   **ALBURY AND RYCOTE**   4m (6¹/₂km)

Maps: OS Sheets Landranger 164; Pathfinder 1117.

A flat and easy walk passing through Rycote Park and by Rycote Chapel.

Start: At 649050, Tiddington Village Hall car park.

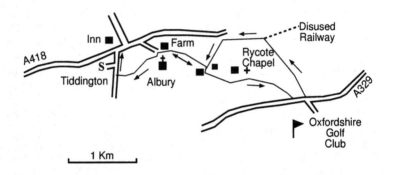

From the entrance to the car park, turn left to reach the A418. Turn right, with care, for 100 yards to reach a minor road on the right, signed for **Albury Church**. Turn right and follow this road to reach Church Farm on the left. Now, bear left along a footpath, go over a stile and walk ahead between barns, the path passing between the farm buildings, on your left, and Albury Church on your right.

Continue ahead along a wide grassy track to reach a house on the right. Here, keep ahead towards a large barn and follow the track as it bends right, then left, through the farmyard. Just past a row of poplars, near a copper beech, turn left through a five-bar metal gate and bear diagonally right across a field towards some trees, following a waymarking arrow. Go over a stile and turn right along a track for 15 yards. Now turn left across a grassy area and head towards the right of **Rycote Chapel**. Rycote Park House will be to your left. Turn right up some steps and follow a path which keeps to the right of the Chapel. Pass to the right of the English Heritage booth and follow the path through the wood.

At a T-junction of tracks, turn right along a wider track. On emerging from the wood bear left across a field, as indicated by the yellow arrow. Over to your left you may catch glimpses of Rycote Lake. At the far side of the field, bear right into a wood, passing between two wooden posts. The wide track bends left across an earth bridge: keep to the main track, but where it bends left, keep ahead along a narrower path. Go over a crossing track and, after another 10 yards, cross a stile on to the A329. Turn left, with care, for 100 yards, then turn left over a stile and small bridge into a field. The entrance to Oxfordshire Golf Club is on the opposite side of the road. Go along the left edge of three fields to reach an embankment. Go up the embankment and turn left at the top to go along a narrow path. The path soon widens into a track: you are now on a disused railway line.

On reaching a crossing track, turn left along the concrete drive and follow it to Home Farm. Here, turn right and retrace your steps to Albury Church and Church Farm. From the entrance to the farm continue along the drive for 60 yards, then bear left down an enclosed path signed for the Oxfordshire Way. Go through a gate and down the left edge of the field beyond. Cross a stile and bridge, then cross fields, following the Oxfordshire Way signs to reach a road.

Turn right along the road and, just before you reach the A418, turn left into the Village Hall car park.

POINTS OF INTEREST:

Church of St Helen, Albury – Albury at one time had a larger community than Tiddington – not so today. The original church was demolished in 1828, the present one being built in 1830 by Thomas Rickman. The font is all that remains of the original building.

Rycote Park and Rycote Chapel – Rycote Park House was built in 1539 by Lord Williams, the founder of Thame Grammar School. On at least six occasions the house was visited by four separate monarchs, including Henry VIII. The house is private, but the Chapel is managed by English Heritage. Built in 1449, it contains a Royal Pew built for Charles I. It is open on Saturdays, Sundays and Bank Holidays from 2pm – 6pm from April 1st until September 30th.

REFRESHMENTS:

The Fox Inn, Tiddington, on the A418 near the start of the walk.

Walk 22   GREAT HASELEY   4m ($6^{1}/_{2}$km)

Maps: OS Sheets Landranger 164; Pathfinder 1117.

A fairly flat walk from a lovely little village dating back to the days of the Doomsday Book.

Start: At 644017, St Peter's Church, Great Haseley.

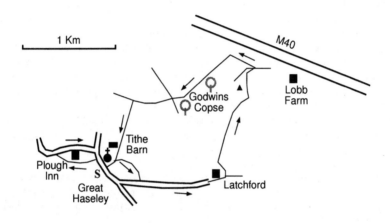

Go through the gate of **St Peter's Church** and follow the path which passes to its right. At the far side, go through a kissing gate and across a track. Go over a stile and straight across the field beyond to reach another stile. Now bear half-right to reach a stile in the right-hand hedge. Cross and go straight across the next field to reach a stile on to a road (Latchford Lane). Turn left and follow the road to Latchford House. Now continue along a bridleway to Latchford Farm. When the metalled surface ends, fork left through a gate, then immediately fork left again to follow the left edge of a field. Go past a stone building and then look for a stile on the left. Go over and bear right across the field beyond to reach a stile in the far corner. Go over the stile and a footbridge, then bear slightly right across a field to reach a gap in the far hedge.

Go through the gap and continue up the right edge of a second field. At the top, follow the field edge around to the left to reach a stile on the right, near a solitary tree. Cross the stile and a footbridge, and head straight across a field to reach the far hedge. There are some good views to the right from here. Turn left along the hedge for 350 yards, noting the trig. point in the field to your left, to reach a farm track. Turn left along the track, but when it bends left, continue straight ahead across a field to reach a stile and footbridge in the bottom hedge. Over to your right you will see, and hear, the traffic on the M40. Immediately after crossing the stile, turn left and follow a path, with a hedge on your left, through three fields. Pass Godwin's Copse, then go over a stile and an L-shaped footbridge.

Now bear left over a rail stile (ignoring the better stile on the right) and turn right up the edge of a field, walking with a hedge on your right. At the top corner, turn left, then almost immediately right along a track, keeping a hedge on your right. Approximately 30 yards short of the field corner, turn left across the field to reach, and cross, a gated culvert. Follow the path beyond uphill, with a hedge on your right, through two fields to reach a recreation ground. Continue along the right edge of the ground to its far corner. Here, go through a gap and walk ahead, passing a **Tithe Barn** and a modern barn in the grounds to the right. About 40 yards further on, turn right through a kissing gate back into the churchyard. Follow the path back, this time to the left of the church, to the front gate.

To extend the walk go through the gate and straight ahead along the road opposite. At the main road, cross, with care, to reach a gate just to the left of the house on the right. Continue along the right edge of a field to reach a stile. Cross and walk ahead along a narrow enclosed path between houses. The path emerges at a road: turn right and follow the road through the village, passing the Plough Inn on the right, to reach a road junction. Turn right, and then take the first turning on the left to return to the church.

POINTS OF INTEREST:

St Peter's Church, Great Haseley – Parts of the church date back to the 12th century. However, the discovery of Roman coins in the churchyard suggests that a settlement has been here since much earlier times. A document in the Bodleian Library, Oxford, shows that a church has stood on the site since AD800. The village is also mentioned in the Doomsday Book.

The Tithe Barn – The barn is thought to date from about 1400.

REFRESHMENTS:

The Plough Inn, Great Haseley.

Walk 23   **LETCOMBE REGIS**   4m ($6\frac{1}{2}$km)

Maps: OS Sheets Landranger 174; Pathfinder 1154.

From the Vale of the White Horse, this walk ascends to the Ridgeway and visits an Iron Age Fort.

Start: At 380864, St Andrew's Church, Letcombe Regis.

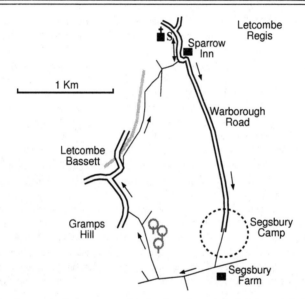

Facing Letcombe Laboratory, with the **church** on your right, turn left along the road, following the sign for 'Village, Downs only', and noting the thatched cottages. Bear right, then left, to reach the Sparrow Inn on the left. Here, turn right along Warborough Road. The road ascends, gently at first, then more steeply, to reach the top of the ridge. Just before the road starts to level out you enter **Segsbury Camp**. After another 50 yards you will reach a stile and gate on both sides of the road. At this point you are almost at the centre of the fort. The boundary of the fort can clearly be seen encircling the area.

    Ignore the stiles, continuing ahead, descending gradually to reach a cross-tracks. The Ridgeway crosses here: turn right along this ancient track for 600 yards, passing a turning on the left, to reach a stile on the right. Go over and cross the middle of the field beyond, descending gradually to reach a stile at the far side. Here, stop and admire the view, looking down at the Letcombes and the Oxfordshire plain beyond. Over to the left you may be able to make out the features of the land form known as the Devil's Punchbowl.

Go over the stile and continue downhill, more steeply now, with woodland on your right. When the woodland ends, go over a stile and follow the left edge of a field to reach a stile and lane (Gramps Hill). Turn right down the lane, following it into the village of **Letcombe Bassett**, passing an attractive thatched barn on the right and a thatched house on the left. On reaching a road junction, bear right following the sign for 'Letcombe Regis 1'.

Go past Downs House, with its many thatched buildings, on the right, and, where the road bends left, go straight on along a footpath which runs just to the left of a garden. (The footpath is signed for 'Circular walk, Letcombe Regis 1'. Follow the path, which at first runs parallel with the road below, then swings gently right, away from the road, which is replaced by Letcombe Brook, which flows through a mini gorge. In Spring the path is attractive with Mayflower, a complete contrast with the earlier ridge walking.

On reaching a gate, bear right along an enclosed path between fences. At the end of the path, bear left along a grassy track, bearing right at a footpath sign to reach a road. The Sparrow Inn is ahead and to the left. To return to the church, turn left and follow the road back through the village.

POINTS OF INTEREST:
St Andrew's Church, Letcombe Regis – A church on this site is mentioned in the Doomsday Book. Parts of the present church date back to the 12th century. In the churchyard a Maori chieftain – George King Hirango – from Wanganui, New Zealand is buried. He died of tuberculosis in 1871, aged 19.
Segsbury Camp – The camp is an Iron Age hillfort. One story has it that a great battle was fought here. The blood flowed down the hillside, while the villagers below shouted 'Let the blood come. Let it come. Let it come', hence the name Letcombe.
Letcombe Bassett – Thomas Hardy based his book *Jude the Obscure* on the village. The cottage where Jude first met Arabella can still be seen down by the brook.

REFRESHMENTS:
The Sparrow Inn, Letcombe Regis.

Walk 24   SHENINGTON AND ALKERTON   4m (6½km)

Maps: OS Sheets Landranger 151; Pathfinder 1021.

An undulating walk in the north-west corner of Oxfordshire, mainly across farmland.

Start: At 371428, the Bell Inn, Shenington.

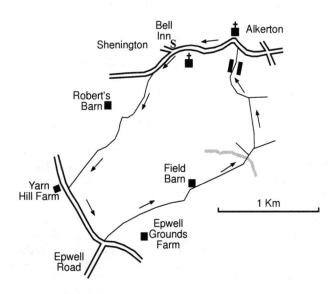

If you use the inn car park, please check with the landlord beforehand. Facing the inn, turn left to reach a road junction. Turn right along the road through the village. Go past 'Mill Land' and 'The Level' on the left. After passing the last house on the left, bear left over a stile just to the right of a gate. Go down the left edge of the field beyond and cross a small stream at the bottom. Continue straight on up the next field to reach a gate in the top left-hand corner. Go through and follow the direction of a yellow arrow waymarker, walking along the left edge of a field.

Go through a gate and then steeply down a slope to reach a gate/gap at the bottom. Go through and bear left across the next field, passing to the right of a pond. Cross a stile and maintain direction across the next field, keeping just to the left of a farm track. Cross a sleeper bridge and, after 20 yards, turn left over a stile in the left-hand hedge. Veer right to cross the next field diagonally to a point just left of the far right corner. Go over a (padded) electric fence and down a slope to cross a footbridge. .

Bear right across the field beyond, passing just to the left of a telegraph pole to reach a stile at the far corner. Epwell Hill can be seen to your right, and not far beyond it is the boundary with Warwickshire. Cross the stile on to a road and turn left to reach a road junction on the right. Here, turn left along a bridleway signed for 'Balscote $1^3/_4$', crossing two fields, keeping to the right of a barn in the second field.

Go through two gates and bear left across the next field. Epwell Grounds Farm is over to the right. At the far side of the field, continue along a farm track, with a hedge on your right. If you stop and look behind you will see four small hills. From left to right these are: Yarn Hill, Epwell Hill, Rough Hill and Shenlow Hill. On reaching a 'No Entry' sign, turn left, with the track, towards some barns. At the first barn, turn right and follow a track across the middle of a field.

Bear left, downhill, across the next field and, at the bottom, go through a gate and cross a footbridge. Now bear slightly left across a field to go through another gate and over an earth bridge. Bear left up a bank and go over a stile to the left of a gate. Continue along the left edge of three fields, with a small stream on your left. Cross a small footbridge and head towards Shenington Church, which you can see on the hill ahead.

The field gets rather boggy, so keep to the higher ground. At the far side, go through the gate on the right, and walk ahead along a path, passing some gardens on the left. Go through a gate, down some steps, and bear left, then right along a gravelled drive and road to reach a road junction. The drive to **Alkerton Church** is directly ahead. To continue the walk, turn left and follow the main road, which descends and ascends, back to Shenington, passing the **church** on the left. The Bell Inn is a little further on, on the right.

POINTS OF INTEREST:

St Michael's Church, Alkerton – This early 13th-century church contains some carvings which are thought to depict the life and times of Edward, the Black Prince. Although small, the church has some large Norman arches. The rectory, nearby, is Jacobean.

Shenington Church – This is the mother church of St Michael's, Alkerton. It has an impressive Tudor tower.

REFRESHMENTS:

The Bell Inn, Shenington.

Walk 25　　　　　**CHADDLEWORTH**　　　　4m (6¹/₂km)

Maps: OS Sheets Landranger 174; Pathfinder 1171.

A fairly level walk across farmland and along country lanes to the north of the village. The walk skirts Spray Wood, which is full of bluebells in springtime.

Start: At 416773, the Ibex Inn, Chaddleworth.

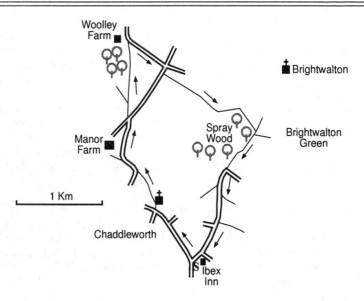

If you use the inn car park, please check with the landlord beforehand. With your back to the inn, turn left (southwards) to reach a road junction. Turn right along the Farnborough road, passing some thatched cottages. At the next junction, continue straight ahead, uphill, and, just past the entrance to Chaddleworth House, turn right along a lane signed 'To the Church'. Go through the gate into the churchyard and follow the path around to the left of St Andrew's Church, heading towards a hedge just right of a large tree. Here, bear right, keeping the hedge on your right, to reach a gate.

Go through and turn left along a track. At the far end, go over a stile and bear right across a field to reach its far corner. Here, go through a gate and walk ahead down a road. Follow the road as it bends right, passing Manor Farm on the left. At a road junction, cross, with care, and continue up the track opposite, passing a barn on the left. At a farm cross-tracks, go through a gate and turn right. Go over an electric fence and head across the field beyond, keeping the wire fence on your right.

At the field corner, turn left along the field for 50 yards, then turn right over a stile waymarked with a yellow arrow. Bear left across two fields to reach a stile in the opposite corner, near Woolley Farm. Cross and turn right along a road to reach a crossroads. Turn right and, after 50 yards, turn left up a farm track, following it to reach a corner of Spray Wood. Follow the track as it bends right, keeping the wood on your right. At the far corner of the wood, at a path junction, turn right, still keeping the wood on your right as you continue along the woodland edge. Over to your left you can see the village of **Brightwalton**.

At the far end of the wood you will emerge on to a road, at a bend: continue straight ahead along the road, following it back to Chaddleworth. About 30 yards after passing a road junction on the left, you will reach the **Ibex Inn**.

POINTS OF INTEREST:
Brightwalton – Seen on the walk, but not visited, this village was once owned by the Wroughton family, who lived at Nearby Woolley Park. In order to pay heavy death duties, however, most of the property was sold off. The village has twice been the winner of its section of 'The Best Kept Village' Competition.

The Ibex Inn – The inn is a Grade 3 listed building. During the 17th century the building consisted of two cottages, being part of a larger farm complex. Before becoming an inn, it was an off-licence and, before that, a bakery.

REFRESHMENTS:
The Ibex Inn, Chaddleworth.

Walk 26   **STRATTON AUDLEY**   4m (6½km)
Maps: OS Sheets Landranger 164; Pathfinder 1070.
Starting along the 'Cross Bucks Way' this fairly level walk
provides distant views of the North Chilterns in Buckinghamshire.
Start: At 608260, the Red Lion Inn, Stratton Audley.

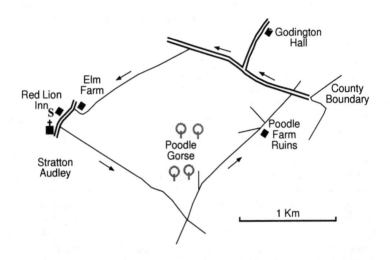

Parking is available in the road close to the inn. With your back to the inn, turn left to
reach a road junction. **Stratton Audley Church** is on your right. Turn right and, after
30 yards, turn left, passing a bench seat. Go over a stile signed 'Cross Bucks Way –
Marsh Gibbon 3' and follow the left edge of a paddock. Cross a stile in the far corner
and continue ahead, walking with a wooden fence on your left. Cross another two
stiles, and a footbridge at the far corner. After crossing another bridge and stile in the
next corner, bear left across the field.

Cross another bridge, then bear right to reach a tree-lined hedge. Here, swing
left along the field edge, keeping the hedge and a ditch on your right. The path turns
right, then left, twice before reaching the far corner. We now leave the Cross Bucks
Way: keeping a fence on your right, turn left up the field edge to reach the next

corner. Now, swing left, with the path, and go through a gap into the next field. Turn right up the field edge to reach a track junction with a gap in the hedge on the right. Turn left towards Poodle Gorse.

After 150 yards, look for a crossing path. Turn right, go over a small wooden bridge and follow the path across the middle of a field. Go over another crossing track and maintain direction, passing to the left of a derelict building (the ruins of Poodle Farm). Go over a farm track and across the middle of another field to reach a road. The county boundary is about 200 yards to the right. However, we turn left along the road, following it for $^3/_4$ mile. Now, look for a footpath on the left signed 'Stratton Audley 1'.

Turn left and follow the direction of the fingerpost, bearing slightly right across the field to reach two stiles and a footbridge in the far right-hand corner. Maintain direction across the next field. At the far corner, do not go through the gate on the right: instead, go through the one directly ahead of you. Carry on along the field edge, keeping a hedge on your right. Go past the entrance to Elm Farm, on the right, to reach a stile in the far corner. Cross and bear right along a boardwalk. Pass between a house and a stream, then go along a short drive to reach a road. Turn left into **Stratton Audley**, following the road back to the village church. Now turn right to return to the Red Lion Inn.

POINTS OF INTEREST:
Stratton Audley Church – Parts of the church date back to Norman times, but substantial restoration work was undertaken during the Victorian era. Inside you will find an octagonal medieval font, a Jacobean pulpit, and the massive tomb of Sir John Borlase who took over the manor house from the Audley family.
Stratton Audley – The village takes its name from the Audley family who owned the Manor House during the 14th century. Coupled with a Roman road which ran from Alchester to Towcester, the name 'Street on Audley' became Stratton Audley.

REFRESHMENTS:
The Red Lion, Stratton Audley.

Walk 27   **HURLEY LOCK**   4m (6$\frac{1}{2}$km)

Maps: OS Sheets Landranger 175; Explorer 3.

A level walk, mostly along the Thames towpath. The route can get muddy in some places.

Start: At 825840, the car park in Hurley village, just opposite the church.

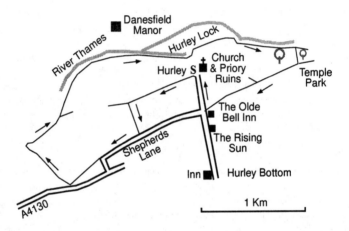

With your back to the **Church of St Mary the Virgin**, leave the car park at the inner left-hand corner. Go along a short enclosed path and over a stile, continuing ahead along the metalled road beyond. To your left are open fields, while over to your right is a caravan park. After 500 yards, just beyond a large oak tree, turn left over a stile. Go along the edge of a field, walking with a hedge on your right, then go over a stile and continue ahead, passing a house, on your left, to reach Shepherd's Lane.

Turn right. After 400 yards, where the lane bends sharp left, carry straight on along a track. Pass to the right of Shepherd's Cottage and, maintaining the same direction, follow a path across the middle of the field to reach a stile in the left-hand hedge. Do not go over the stile onto the A4130: instead, turn half-right across the same field and, at the far side, go over a stile in the hedge and maintain direction, across the next field, heading for the rear of the second white house from the left.

Go over a stile and follow the concrete path beyond, walking with a brick wall on your right to reach a gate at the side of the house. Go through and continue along the edge of the front lawn to reach the River Thames. Turn right along the tow-path. After passing a small cottage, 'Poisson Duc', on the right, go through a gap next to a gate, and bear left along the river-bank. On the other side of the river, high up on the hill, you can see Danesfield Manor, a large attractive building which is now an hotel.

At this point the River Thames makes a sweeping right-hand bend: you can either keep to the bank, or go across the meadow, cutting off the bend. Either way you will eventually reach a weir. Opposite the weir, go through a stileway, leaving the meadow through a small iron gate. Go over a small wooden bridge, continuing ahead to reach a larger bridge, over the Thames. If you wish, you can turn right at this point and follow a path back to the start.

To continue the walk, turn left, over the bridge, then turn right past Hurley Lock. Continue ahead, beyond the lock, to reach another wooden bridge over the Thames. Cross this and turn left along the tow-path, walking with the river on your left and a meadow on your right. At the far side of the meadow, go through a gate, and continue ahead, now with some private woodland on your right. After 150 yards, look for a path, on the right, which goes through the wood.

Turn right and follow this narrow, enclosed path to reach a farm drive at Temple Park. Turn right and follow a path across the flat riverside meadows. Cross a lane near a caravan park, and continue along the signed path opposite. The path emerges at Hurley High Street, just to the right of **The Olde Bell Inn**: turn right and follow the road back to Hurley Church. The car park will be on your left.

POINTS OF INTEREST:

Church of St Mary the Virgin – The church is an odd shape, in that it is long, narrow and tall. It is thought to have been the nave of an old Saxon Priory, the ruins of which are situated behind the building. Behind the flint and brick wall is a dovecote built by monks in about 1306, and an old tithe barn which has been converted into a private residence.

The Olde Bell Inn – The inn dates from 1135 and is considered to be the oldest coaching inn in England.

REFRESHMENTS:

The Olde Bell Inn, Hurley.
The Rising Sun, Hurley.

Walk 28   **ISLIP** $4^{1}/_{4}$m $(6^{3}/_{4}$km)

Maps: OS Sheets Landranger 164; Pathfinder 1092.

An easy walk from the ancient village of Islip, across fields recorded in the Doomsday Book, and a visit to the interesting church at Woodeaton.

Start: At 527140, the car park opposite the Swan Inn, Islip.

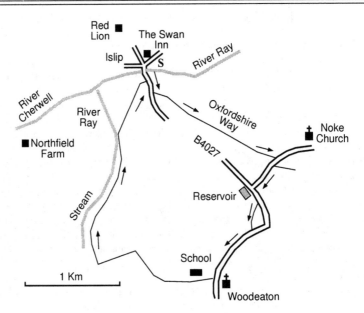

Leave the car park and turn left, then immediately left again over the River Ray. Follow the road up to the top of the hill. There, turn left along a concrete track signed for the Oxfordshire Way. After 20 yards, bear right along a track through some allotments. Cross a stile and go along the right edge of field. Cross a second stile and go across the middle of the next three fields. At the far side of the third field, cross a stile and go along a hedged path, which opens out with a field on the right. Cross a stile and head down a tree-lined path to reach a road. Turn right, up the road. There are views left towards Beckley and the radio mast from here. At a road junction – the grassy mound of Noke Reservoir is just opposite – cross the B4027, with care, and turn left along the grass verge. After 50 yards, turn right to pass a broken stile and bear diagonally left across some scrubby grass, and then across a field, to reach a stile on to a road. Turn right and follow the road into Woodeaton.

Just before you reach the **Church of the Holy Rood**, you pass a small village green on the left and the castle-like walls of the Council Offices on the right. At the corner of the Council Office wall, near the church, turn right, through a gate, and follow a footpath, signed 'Cutterslowe $2^1/_4$'. On reaching a track junction, turn right along a grassy track and, when the track ends, at an open field, turn left along the field edge. In the distance, to your left, you can see the buildings of Radcliffe Hospital, sited on the hill above Oxford. At the field corner you will reach a small stream: turn right along the field edge, keeping the stream on your left. Across the field, on the other side of the stream, you can see Water Eaton Manor. At the next field corner, bear right with the field edge. The River Cherwell is now on your left. Cross a stile in next field corner and go along the bank of the river for $^1/_2$ mile.

Go over a stile and up a bank. Islip Church comes into view ahead: maintain direction to reach the field corner, turning right there to walk alongside the wire fence. After 50 yards, turn left over a stile and go diagonally right across the field. Cross a stile and go along the left edge of the next field. Pass some allotments, on the right, then go between houses to reach a road. Turn left to return to the car park.

POINTS OF INTEREST:

Islip – The village has a long history. Edward the Confessor was born here in about AD1003. The three fields you cross early in the walk were once a huge pasture, called Cow Pasture, which is recorded in the Doomsday Book.

Church of The Holy Rood, Woodeaton – The church, built in the early 13th century, contains a 14th-century wall painting. The church also has another unusual feature, in that the tower is built inside.

REFRESHMENTS:

The Swan Inn, Islip.

The Red Lion, Islip.

Please note that the inn marked on the OS map in Noke village is now closed.

Walk 29   SWALCLIFFE $4^{1}/_{4}$m ($6^{3}/_{4}$km)

Maps: OS Sheets Landranger 151; Pathfinder 1044.

A fairly level rural walk from the ancient village of Swalcliffe, heading south to an Iron Age Fort, at Tadmarton Heath, returning via Tadmarton.

Start: At 378378, the Church of St Peter and St Paul, Swalcliffe.

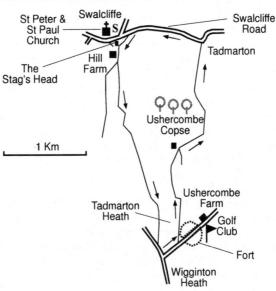

With your back to the church, turn left along the B4035. Go past a turning on the left, signed for Swalcliffe Lea, and, after 75 yards, turn right, across the road, to reach a narrow, enclosed footpath heading down through trees. Cross a bridge over a small stream and turn right along the bank. Cross a stile at the far end and bear left across a field to reach a gate. Go through and bear right across the next field to reach another gate just to the left of Hill Farm. Turn left along a farm track and go through another gate.

   Continue along the right edge of two fields and, on entering a third field, bear slightly left to reach a gate about 50 yards to the left of the far right-hand corner. Go through and bear left along a faint path across the middle of the next field. At the far side, go through a gap in the hedge and maintain direction across the next field. It can be muddy here. Go through another gap and continue ahead, passing just to the right of a small copse. In the next field, bear diagonally right to reach a road at Tadmarton Heath.

Turn left, passing a house on the left to a road junction. Here, turn left for 300 yards to reach a gate and path on the left, signed 'Pidleway/Tadmarton'. Go through the gate and note the bank on the right: it forms parts of the ramparts of an **Iron Age Fort**. In fact, the road you have just left runs right through the centre of the fort. Continue to the middle of the field, from where there is a good view ahead, then bear left to reach the far left-hand corner.

Go through a gate and along the edge of two fields. In the second field the track bends left, then right, still following the field edge: after 50 yards, bear left, slightly away from the field edge, to reach a farm gate near a couple of small trees. Continue along the left edge of a field and, when some farm buildings come into view, down in a dip, bear right to reach a farm gate just to the right of the buildings. Go through and turn right up a bank. After 200 yards, bear left into a small valley and cross towards some trees in the right-hand corner of the field.

In the corner you will join a farm track: follow it through the belt of trees and up the hill on the other side. Go through a gate and continue along the farm track, which bends right across a couple of fields before reaching some houses and a road at Tadmarton. Turn left along the road (the B4035), following it, with care - keep to the verge and in single file if you are a group - back to the start at Swalcliffe.

POINTS OF INTEREST:
The Church of St Peter and St Paul, Swalcliffe – A church has stood on the mound overlooking the village since Saxon times. It was altered and enlarged during the 14th century and further improved during the Victorian era. The church has some beautiful stained glass windows.
Iron Age Fort, Tadmarton Heath – Evidence of human habitation has been found on the site dating back 1300 years. The road which bisects the camp follows the line of a prehistoric way, one used by Welsh drovers until the 19th century.

REFRESHMENTS:
The Stag's Head, Swalcliffe.
The Lampet Arms, Tadmarton.

Walk 30   BUSCOT AND KELMSCOT $4^{1}/_{2}$m ($7^{1}/_{4}$km)

Maps: OS Sheets Landranger 163; Pathfinder 1135.

A flat walk visiting the village of Kelmscott once the country home of the designer William Morris. Muddy in wet conditions.

Start: At 230977, the National Trust car park at Buscot Weir.

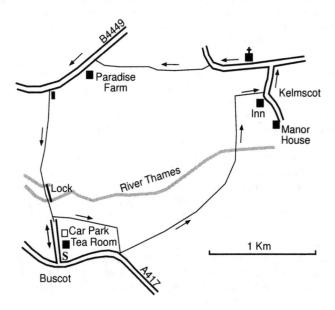

From the main entrance to the car park, turn down the lane (signed 'To the Weir'). When the lane bends left, turn right along the left side of a ditch. Cross a wooden bridge and go along the right edge of the field beyond. At a gap in the hedge, on the right, continue straight on to reach a gap at the field corner. Here, bear slightly right and then go along the left edge of the next field to reach an iron gate.

    Go through and turn right along a wide track. Just before reaching a road (the A417) turn left through a gate and head diagonally left across a field. Go through a gap and cross the next field towards two tall trees. Cross a footbridge and turn right into the adjoining field. Immediately turn left and follow the left edge of the field, keeping the hedgerow to your left.

At the field corner, do not go through the gap ahead: instead, turn right, then left, still following the field edge, to reach a footbridge/stile on the left. Cross and bear right across a field, following the direction of the signpost towards a distant white building. When you reach a track, turn left to reach a Private car park. Cross a stile, go through the car park and over a stone bridge. Turn left, then right across a bridge over the River Thames. On the far side, turn right over a stile, then immediately turn left along the field edge, heading away from the river. At the field corner, cross two footbridges and veer left into the left-hand field. Turn right, keeping the field edge on your right, and, at the field corner, turn right along a grassy path between hedgerows to reach road. The Plough Inn and **Kelmscot Manor** are to the right here.

Turn left along the road to reach a T-junction. Turn left, passing a church on the right. Now, when the road bends right, continue ahead through a gap into a field, just to the right of a gravel track. Bear slightly right across the field to reach a footbridge (the Oxfordshire/Gloucestershire Boundary). Cross and continue ahead across the next field to reach a corner. Go over a stile and continue with a hedge on the right. Go through a gate and walk ahead across the next field, keeping to the right of Paradise Farm to reach a road.

Turn left along the road for 500 yards, then, just past Greenacres, turn left along a track. Go through the farmyard and continue towards a line of trees. On reaching the tree and a stream, turn right, go over a stile, and, after another 20 yards, turn left and cross two bridges. Beyond the second bridge, bear left across a field, heading towards a brick building to reach the Thames. Turn left along the towpath and cross the Thames at **Buscot** Lock. On reaching the Thames Water Works, turn left along a track and follow it back to the National Trust car park.

POINTS OF INTEREST:

Buscot – Considered to be the most north-westerly village in Berkshire, most of the parish and village of Buscot is owned by the National Trust. An 18th-century stately home, Buscot Park, is situated about a mile south-east of the village.

Kelmscott Manor – Built in 1871, this was once the summer home of William Morris, who became well known as a designer of tapestries, wallpaper, furniture and books. He is buried in the churchyard of Kelmscott Church. The house is only open on Wednesdays, from 1st April – 30th September, between the hours of 11am – 1pm and 2pm – 5pm.

REFRESHMENTS:
The Plough Inn, Kelmscott.
The Village Shop in Buscot serves tea.

Maps: OS Sheets Landranger 175; Explorer 3.

A contrasting walk in the South Chilterns hills, can get muddy in parts during wet weather.

Start: At 675877, the Crown Inn, Nuffield Common, on the A4130.

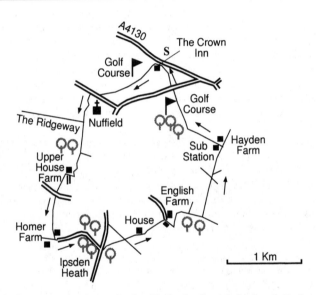

If you use the inn car park, please check with the landlord beforehand. Facing the A4130, turn left, passing the inn and telephone box, and head up the track which runs parallel with the road. When the track ends, continue ahead between a house and outbuildings to reach the edge of Huntercombe Golf Course. Follow the line of white numbered marker posts across the course and, after passing through a small wood, veer left across the next fairway, heading towards the clubhouse. Just before the clubhouse, bear right through a gap in the hedge and bear left across a field to a stile in the far corner. Cross on to a road, just opposite **Nuffield Church**. Turn right for 110 yards, then go left along the field edge, as signed for the Ridgeway. At the far corner, go through a kissing gate and walk downhill, through trees. Now, where the

Ridgeway turns right, go ahead over a stile, still descending. On emerging from the trees, go ahead along the field edge to reach an old iron stile in the field corner. Follow the path beyond as it bends right, then left, passing a small pond on the right, to reach the drive of Upper House Farm. Cross the drive, go over the stile opposite, and along the field edge for 55 yards to reach a fingerpost. Turn left across a field to reach a road. Cross and maintain direction across the field opposite. Go over a stile and follow a line of telegraph poles, aiming just to the right of a small copse. In the field corner, go over a stile, cross a drive and go between Homer Farm, on the left, and a barn on the right. Descend to reach a road just opposite The Old Farmhouse. Turn left and follow the road through a wood, to reach a road junction.

Cross the road and bear left along a path through the trees opposite. Cross a track and walk ahead for a few yards to a stile. Cross and go along the right edge of the field beyond. When the enclosure on the right ends, go ahead across a field, following a line of posts to reach a stile in the field corner. Cross the stile, the road beyond and another stile opposite, and bear right across the next field to reach a stile near a clump of trees. Cross and go between a tennis court, on the right, and a hedge on the left to reach a drive. Turn left and follow the drive as it bends right, but when it turns left towards a house, go straight ahead, over a cattle-grid and along the track to English Farm. Turn right between barns and, just after passing the barn on the left, turn left over a stile and follow a track as it bends left around the farm. Keep to the track as it bends right, downhill at first, then uphill. At the brow of Barley Hill turn left over a stile and go along the left edge of the field beyond to reach a gate and a crossing track. Turn left and follow the track towards Hayden Farm.

Shortly after passing an electric sub-station turn left between barns. Go over a stile and walk along the field edge. (**Grim's Ditch** is on the right here.) Cross the next two fields and, at the wood edge on the left, veer right to a stile in the opposite corner. Go over and veer right across the golf course fairway, heading towards a red post. Now maintain direction to reach a road. Cross and go ahead through a thin line of trees, veering left across the next fairway to return to the start.

POINTS OF INTEREST:

Nuffield Church – William Morris, Viscount Nuffield, the well-known car manufacturer is buried in the church grounds, on the left just before the church.
Grim's Ditch – This ancient earthwork is easily missed as it looks like an ordinary ditch and bank.

REFRESHMENTS:
The Crown Inn, Nuffield Common.

Walk 32   **BOWSEY AND ASHLEY HILLS**   4¹/₂m (7¹/₄km)

Maps: OS Sheets Landranger 175; Pathfinder 1157; Explorer 3.

Two wood-covered hills with interesting varieties of plants and flowers.

Start: At 822794, a lay-by on the A4, Knowl Hill, near the Seven Stars Inn.

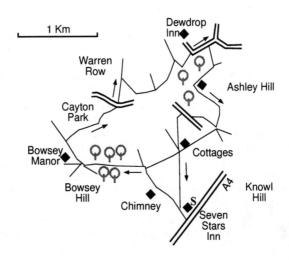

Go up Star Lane, to the left of the inn, to reach a small green. Here the track veers left and becomes unsurfaced: follow it for 440 yards to reach a track junction. Turn left along a wide track into a wood, ascending gradually to the top of **Bowsey Hill**. At the top, at a junction of tracks, follow the track to the right, passing the entrance to Bowsey Manor on the left. Just before reaching the first house on the right, turn right through a wooden gate and follow a narrow path, downhill, through wooded Cayton Park. At the bottom, the track widens and eventually emerges on to a road at Warren Row. Turn right along the road for 50 yards. At 'Hill View', turn left along a drive between houses. When the drive ends, go ahead along a footpath which becomes enclosed. There are good views ahead towards the South Chilterns. At a Christmas tree, bear right, away from the left-hand fence, to reach a stile. Cross and drop down to a sunken path. Turn right and follow the path to reach a bridleway/path junction. Here, turn left up the bridleway. Ignore the turn on the left, continuing straight ahead, as directed by a footpath sign. Keep to the main track as it bends left, through a gate, to reach a stile. Go over and walk along the left edge of a field to reach a stile in the far corner. Cross and go down a small wooden ramp to reach a footpath. Turn right along this enclosed path, ascending gradually and bending left to reach a path junction. Turn left along the broader path to reach a road. Turn left here to reach the Dewdrop Inn.

The route continues along the road and, just before reaching a road junction, turns right along a footpath, ascending fairly steeply up **Ashley Hill**. Go straight over at a cross-tracks and continue to climb to reach a drive. Turn right towards a house, but, just before reaching the gates, turn right, then left, following the house boundary around to reach a broad track. Turn left, still with the house on your left. The path levels out and soon starts to descend, with a good view ahead. Go straight across two cross-tracks to reach a stile at the edge of a wood. Cross and walk ahead with a hedge on your right. Go through a gate and maintain direction, but now with a hedge on your left. Cross a stile and continue to another stile in the field corner, at a footpath junction.

Do not cross the stile: instead, turn right, as directed by a footpath sign, crossing the field to reach another stile in the far corner. Cross and turn left to reach a road. Turn right for 80 yards, then cross the road to reach a footpath through a wood. At the far side of the wood, cross a stile into a field and turn right. Cross a stile by a gate, and go half-left across the next field to reach a stile in the far corner, near a bungalow. Cross and turn left to a T-junction of paths. Turn left, over a stile, and then, just in front of the bungalow, turn right over a stile into a field. Head down across the middle of the field, aiming just to the right of some red brick houses. At the bottom of the field, cross a stile and walk past the houses to rejoin Star Lane. Now follow the lane back to the start.

POINTS OF INTEREST:
Bowsey Hill – The hill is noted for its London Clay, hence the nearby tile works. The woods contain a rich variety of trees and plants.
Ashley Hill – The hill is managed by the Forestry Commission, as is Lots Wood. The area is rich in flora and is also interesting geologically. Glacial sand and gravel exist on this hilltop. There is a trig. point in the grounds of the house at the summit.

REFRESHMENTS:
The Seven Stars, Knowl Hill.
The Dewdrop Inn, north side of Ashley Hill.

Walk 33   BEENHAM AND DOUAI ABBEY $4^1/_2$m ($7^1/_4$km)

Maps: OS Sheets Landranger 174; Pathfinder 1187.

Two churches and an Abbey, plus some good views over the Kennet valley gives this walk plenty of interest.

Start: At 594689, the Stocks Inn, Beenham.

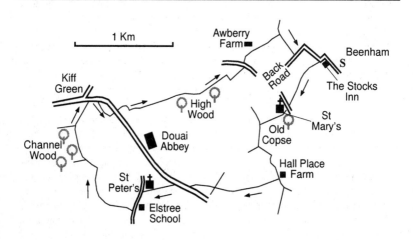

If you use the inn car park, please check with the landlord beforehand. From the inn, turn left along the road but, at a sharp right-hand bend, continue ahead into Stoneyfield Road. After 25 yards bear left along a track. When the main track bends left, go straight on down a narrow path. Soon you will have views, to the left, over the Kennet valley. The path emerges just opposite the lych-gate of **St Mary's Church**. Go through the lych-gate and walk to the left of the church to reach a stile in the churchyard corner. Cross and bear right across a field to reach a wood (Old Copse). Enter the wood and go down a fairly steep path. At the far end of the wood, cross a stile and turn left down a wide track. The track bends left, then right, and ascends towards Hall Place Farm. At the top of the rise, just past a barn on the left, turn sharp right up a slope and go through a gate. Bear half-left across the field beyond, heading towards the left side of some trees. Cross a stile by a gate, and continue along the edge of the next field to reach a stile on right. Cross and follow a winding path through woodland to reach a cross-tracks at the far side.

Go through the squeeze stile opposite and follow yellow arrow waymarkers across three fields to reach a road in the far corner of the third. Turn right for 30 yards, then fork left, over a drive, to reach a playing field. Turn left and follow the field edge, with trees on your left, to reach the corner. Now maintain direction, crossing a field towards the spire of St Peter's Church. Go through the churchyard to reach a road and turn left, passing Elstree School. Just after the playing field on the right, turn right through a swing gate and go down a grassy track. Go past ponds on the left, then cross two stiles each side of a woodland strip. Turn right along a field edge and, shortly after a left bend, turn right, through a gateway, to enter Channel Wood on a wide track. Turn right at a path junction to reach a field. Turn left up the field edge, with the wood on your left and, at the top corner, turn right, still following the field edge. At the next corner, turn left along a broad track to reach a road at Kiff Green.

Turn right for 100 yards, then, just beyond some farm buildings, turn right over a stile and cross the field beyond to the opposite corner. Cross a stile and footbridge to reach a road. Cross the stile opposite and turn right to follow the edge of field, walking parallel to the road and with a good view of **Douai Abbey**. Cross a stile in the corner and turn left along a wide track. Go ahead into the next field, now with a hedge and playing field on the right. At a path junction, go straight on into a wood. Leave the wood along a gravel path between fences, to reach a lane at some houses. Turn right for 50 yards, then left along a tarmac path to reach road. Turn left and, after the last terraced house on the right, turn right along a narrow path. Go over a stile and cross a field, passing to the right of Awberry Farm. Go across the next two fields, following the hedge on the left and, just before the end of the second field, turn left over a stile and go through woodland to reach a drive at a corner. Turn right and follow the drive to a road (Back Lane). Turn left along the road to return to the Stocks Inn.

POINTS OF INTEREST:
St Mary's Church, Beenham – Inside there is a memorial to Sir Charles Hopson who was responsible for much of the woodwork in St Paul's Cathedral.
Douai Abbey – There has been a Roman Catholic school here since 1855, but in 1903 Benedictine Monks, expelled from France, established an abbey and a school. The site is open to the public.

REFRESHMENTS:
The Stocks Inn, Beenham.

Walk 34   **STOKE ROW** $4\frac{1}{2}$m ($7\frac{1}{4}$km)

Maps: OS. Sheets Landranger 175; Explorer 3.

An undulating walk through attractive woodlands in the South Chiltern Hills. It can be muddy in places during wet weather.

Start: At 685841, the Recreation Ground car park, Stoke Row.

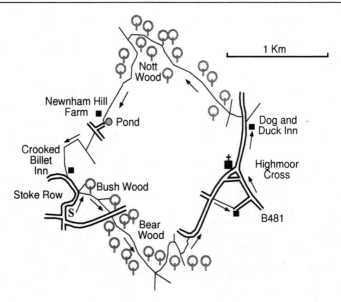

From the car park, go along the left edge of the playing field and, in the far corner, enter Bush Wood through a gap in the hedge. After 10 yards, turn right and, with the playing field on your right, follow a path to reach a road just to the left of Clare Cottage. Cross the road, with care, and go up the bridleway opposite. In Bear Wood, the path ascends, descends, then ascends again, bearing right, to reach an earth bank. Here, turn left for 20 yards to reach a fence corner. Now bear slightly left (look for the white arrow waymarkers) for 200 yards to reach a cross-tracks. Turn left, downhill, following the path as it bends left, then right, to reach a wide gravel track. Turn right, uphill, for 100 yards, then go left over a stile and head downhill along a path which runs just inside the left edge of a wood. At the bottom, turn left along an enclosed path, which swings right to reach a road on a bend. Continue ahead, uphill, along the road to reach a junction on the left. Opposite this road, turn right over a stile and follow an enclosed path. Now go along the left edge of a field to reach a stile on to a lane. Continue straight along the lane, which bends left to reach the B481. Turn left, with care, along the B481 to reach the road junction at Highmoor Cross. Continue along the B481, heading towards Nettlebed, to reach the Dog and Duck Inn on the right.

After a further 100 yards, turn left along the drive of Appletree Cottage. After about 10 yards, bear right along a path between hedges. Cross a stile and go along the left edge of a field. Cross a stile into a wood and immediately fork right. At a path junction, turn right for 20 yards, then bear left along path H2. Cross a drive, continuing along the path opposite, swinging left to reach a stile waymarked with a yellow arrow. Cross and go along the left edge of a field. Cross a stile in the corner and bear left to cross a second stile. Now turn right through a wood to reach a stile at the far side. Cross and go down the field edge, keeping to the left of a wire fence, to reach a stile into Nott Wood. Cross and bear right along a path which gradually ascends through the wood, bending left to reach a wide track. Here, turn left for 440 yards, then, just before a field on the right, turn right along a path, just inside the edge of the wood, to reach a stile in the far corner. Cross and go along the right edge of a field to reach Newnham Hill Farm. Go through a gate on to a lane which bends left, passing a pond on the left, to reach a fork. Turn right, downhill, and, at the next fork, go straight across and down an enclosed path through woodland to reach a road in the valley bottom. Turn right for 40 yards, then turn left to go through two gates in Bush Wood. Now go straight up through a paddock to a stile in the top hedge. Cross this and the field beyond to reach Nottwood Lane, just to the right of the **Crooked Billet Inn**.

Turn left along the lane to reach a sharp right-hand bend. Here, go straight ahead into a wood, and, after 10 yards, turn right, through a gap to return to the playing field passed early in the walk. Now retrace your steps back to the car park.

POINTS OF INTEREST:
Stoke Row – The village is situated on the highest ground in the South Chiltern Hills, approximately 670 feet above sea level. During the 1600s, the area had a thriving tile, brick and pottery industry. During the mid-19th century chair leg bodgers and tent peggers existed in the area. The outbuildings of the **Crooked Billet Inn** were used by the bodgers and peggers. The village is also noted for its cherry trees.

REFRESHMENTS:
The Dog and Duck Inn, Highmoor.
The Crooked Billet Inn, Stoke Row.

Walk 35   **WEST ILSLEY** $4^1/_2$m ($7^1/_4$km)

Maps: OS Sheets Landranger 174; Pathfinder 1155.

*A gentle walk up on to the Berkshire Downs, from a village well
known for its horse racing connections. A typical English village
designated as a conservation area.*

Start: At 471826, the Harrow Inn, West Ilsley.

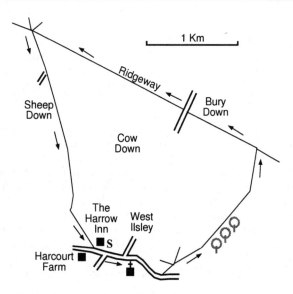

Parking is available close to the inn. With your back to the inn, turn left and follow
the road through the village of **West Ilsley** to reach a road junction. Cross and continue
ahead, passing the church on your right. Just as you leave the village, bear left along
a track (signposted as a cart track), following it past some attractive cottages. At a
fork, bear right along a track which gradually ascends the hillside. As you ascend
there are some good views to your left and behind.

    Near the top of the ridge a track joins from the right. Here, you should veer left.
On your right you will see one of the many racehorse gallops which are a prominent
feature of this area. As you pass between two white posts you actually cross the border
from Berkshire into Oxfordshire: continue ahead, descending gradually to reach a

very wide cross track, the Ridgeway. Ahead you have a panoramic view of the South Oxfordshire plain, while below you can look down on the village of Chilton, the Atomic Energy buildings of Harwell, the cooling towers of Didcot Power Station and watch the traffic on the busy A34.

Turn left along the Ridgeway. You will now stay on this ancient track for the next $1^3/_4$ miles, going over Bury Down and crossing a minor road. Just before the track starts to ascend towards a distant copse you reach a crossing track: turn left between two white posts, then bear left and continue along the left edge of a wide gallop, following the line of a finger post.

Where the gallop veers off to the right, continue straight ahead along a bridleway, walking with a wire fence on the right. Follow the bridleway as it, eventually, descends and turns left to reach a road. There are some good views of the undulating countryside as you descend. At the road, turn left, reaching, after 50 yards, the Harrow Inn, on the left.

POINTS OF INTEREST:

West Ilsley – The village, and surrounding area, have been involved in training racehorse winners, including those owned by the Queen, for many years. Near the entrance to the church is a seat commemorating the fact that *Brigadier Gerard* was trained in the village between 1969 and 1972. *Nasawan*, who won the Derby in 1989, was also trained in the area. Inside the Harrow Inn there is a photo of *Dunfermline*, the horse which won the Oaks and St Leger in the 1970s.

The Morland family established a brewery in the village in 1711, bringing work for the local people. The brewery is now in Abingdon.

REFRESHMENTS:
The Harrow Inn, West Ilsley.

Walk 36   **MORTIMER** $4^1/_2$m ($7^1/_4$km)

Maps: OS Sheets Landranger 175; Pathfinder 1188.

A fairly level walk crossing over the Hampshire border to visit the well-preserved ruins of a Roman Amphitheatre.

Start: At 654646, the Church of St John the Evangelist, Mortimer.

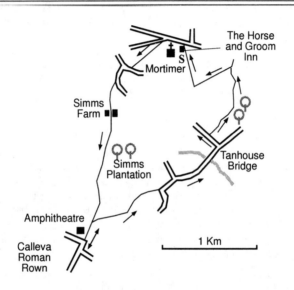

With your back to the church, turn left along West End Road. After 100 yards, turn left into St Johns Road and, after 40 yards, turn right along a narrow, hedged, unmade road. At a junction, bear right to reach Drury Lane. Turn right to reach the next road junction, turning left there to go along Turks Lane. At the next junction, go straight ahead along a 'No Through Road' (Simms Farm Lane). When the tarmac ends, continue along a gravel bridleway, going through Simms Farm.

Continue ahead down a sunken path. Ignore a path going left, continuing along the main track which crosses a small brook. Go through a gate and bear left across a field to reach a stile at the edge of a wood. Cross the stile and a wooden bridge and go ahead up the path beyond, walking through Nine Acres Copse. Go over a crossing track and the stile opposite, then follow the path through a plantation.

At the far side, pass a broken stile and bear left across the middle of a field. Cross a stile and bear right across the next field, passing under electricity wires. Cross a bridge and a stile, then bear left up and across the next field to reach, and go through, a squeeze stile in the left-hand fence. Now turn right up a track, following it to reach a road at a bend. The **Roman Amphitheatre** is on the right. (To visit the walls of the old Roman town of Calleva, continue down the road for 400 yards, returning to this point.)

From the Amphitheatre, retrace your steps down the track, passing the squeeze stile you crossed earlier. Now stay on the track to reach a road. Continue straight ahead along the road to reach a road junction. Carry straight on, following the road as it bends right and passing Tanhouse Cottage, on the left. At the next road junction, turn left for 200 yards, then, just opposite some houses on left, turn right along a path, following it across a field to a wood.

Follow the path, which bends left, through the wood, emerging from the wood along a fenced path near a house called 'Ashfield'. Continue ahead up the drive and, at the top, just before a house on the right, turn sharp left along a track to reach an open field. Turn right along the field edge. After 150 yards, fork right towards the fence and follow the path over a make-shift bridge. Now go along a narrow enclosed path to reach an unmade road. Turn right to reach a cross-roads. Turn left to reach a T-junction, turning right to reach the main road (The Street) in **Mortimer**. Now, turn left, past the Horse and Groom Inn, to return to the church.

POINTS OF INTEREST:

Roman Amphitheatre – This impressive site is almost 2000 years old. Until 1979 the area was just a tall oval embankment surrounded by shrubs. The banks were capable of seating up to 3000 people. The arena, it is thought, was used mainly as a ceremonial site rather than for fighting, as no human bones have been found during excavation. Calleva, must have been quite a site in its day. Walking along part of the walls give you a good idea of its size. It is well worth a visit.

Mortimer – The village dates back to pre-Roman times. The Welsh Drovers came to the village every May and November, when the Mortimer Horse and Welsh Cattle Fairs were held. Present day Mortimer, however, dates mainly from the 19th and 20th centuries.

REFRESHMENTS:

The Horse and Groom Inn, Mortimer.

Walk 37   **DONNINGTON CASTLE** $4^{1}/_{2}$m ($7^{1}/_{4}$km)

Maps: OS Sheets Landranger 174; Pathfinder 1171 and 1187.

This walk, which has one or two short ascents/descents, visits the ruins of a medieval castle and the picturesque Watermill Theatre.

Start: At 463710, the Snelsmore Common Country Park car park.

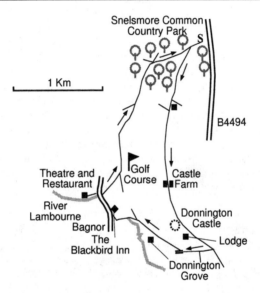

From the entrance to the car park, with your back to the road, take the path on the left, passing a couple of fire beaters. After 20 yards, at a cross-tracks, turn right and go along the main track for the next 200 yards, following the blue arrow waymarkers. At a fork, bear left along a bridleway. Continue straight on at the next cross-tracks to reach a barrier, just before a cottage on the left.

Go ahead, past the barrier and the cottage, following a fenced track. At a track junction, continue straight on, passing a golf course on the right. Carry on through the farmyard of Castle Farm. **Donnington Castle** is now directly ahead of you. Go through a farm gate and follow the track beyond downhill. When you are in line with the castle, turn right, through a gate, into the castle grounds.

There are good views of Newbury and the surrounding countryside from the hilltop. From the castle, the path descends to a car park. Go through the car park and along a minor road, with a wooden fence on your left. Further on you will go down an avenue of trees and pass between stone pillars by Castle Lodge: after another 10 yards turn right along a narrow path, following it to a footpath junction. Continue straight on, and, at the far end, bear slightly right on a path which runs almost parallel to an estate road. Cross a drive and continue ahead, keeping to the left edge of the golf course. Pass Donnington Grove, on the left: soon you will be able to catch glimpses of the River Lambourn, between the trees to your left. When you arrive at a footpath junction, bear left to reach a gate.

Go through and turn right along a gravelled drive, to reach a road near the Blackbird Inn. Bear right along the road and, after crossing a small road bridge, turn left to visit the idyllic setting of the Watermill Theatre and Restaurant at Bagnor. Retrace your steps to the road bridge and turn right over the bridge. After 30 yards, turn left up a path between houses, then go across the middle of a field.

At the top of the rise, cross a stile and turn left along a tree-lined path, following it to reach a farm road. Here, continue ahead to pass a house and garages on the right. The track now ascends fairly steeply under power lines to reach a ridge. Continue ahead, passing under more power lines, where there is a path junction. Carry straight on to reach, and cross, a concrete cross-track. Continue across a muddy clearing, then cross a second concrete track. Continue ahead to reach a path junction. Go straight on for 50 yards, then turn left into the car park. To return to the start, turn right along the exit road.

POINTS OF INTEREST:
Donnington Castle – With the exception of Windsor, Donnington is the only medieval castle of note in Berkshire. It was built in the early 14th century. During the Civil War it was held for the King by Sir John Boys, who took over command two days after the battle of Newbury in 1643. What is now left of the castle is maintained by English Heritage.

REFRESHMENTS:
The Blackbird Inn, Bagnor.

WROXTON   4¹/₂m (7¹/₄km)
or 6m (9¹/₂km)

Maps: OS Sheets Landranger 151; Pathfinder 1022 and 1045.
An undulating walk from one of the prettiest villages in Oxfordshire.
Start: At 414418, the Wroxton Village Pond.

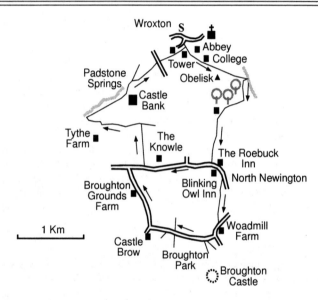

Parking is possible close to the pond. With your back to the pond, cross the road towards the entrance to **Wroxton College**. Go up Dark Lane, to the right of the entrance, and, after 100 yards, turn left along an enclosed path sign 'Banbury 3'. Go through a swing gate and turn left along the left edge of a field. You have a good view of the College on the left. On the hill to your right is a tower, another relic of the old priory. At the far side of the field, go through a gate (not the kissing gate to the right) and turn left to go steeply down the field towards the left edge of a pond. Go through a gate and continue ahead, passing the pond, on your right, to reach a stile. Go over and bear left up a field. Cross a fence stile and head for an obelisk. From it, continue across a field on a well-defined path. At the far side, do not cross the bridge over a stream:

instead, turn right for 20 yards, then go right again towards the corner of a wood. Just before the wood, turn left through a gap and continue along the right edge of a field, with the wood on your right. Follow the woodland edge to reach a farm track, with a farm on your right. Turn left, following the track up, then down, to reach a road at North Newington.

The shorter walk turns right, following the road for $^3/_4$ mile, passing first a road junction, then the entrance to 'The Knowle' on the right. About 250 yards further on, turn right through gate, rejoining the longer walk.

The longer walk turns left, passing the Blinking Owl Inn on the right and the Roebuck Inn on the left. After another 200 yards, just before leaving the village, turn right along a short track between houses. Go through a gate and bear left up a field. Go over a farm track and along a hedge track. When the hedge ends on the right, continue along the left edge of a field to reach a stile. Go over and turn left along a field edge to reach a road. Turn right. At a road junction, bear right and follow the road, with Broughton Park on the left. At the next junction, bear right and follow a track which bends right, passing Broughton Grounds Farm on the left, to reach a road. Turn right for 250 yards, then turn left through a gate, rejoining the shorter walk.

Go up the right edge of two fields and, at the top, go through a gate and along a path which bends left just inside the edge of a wood. At the far end, bear right through a gate and turn left to go through a second gate. Go along the left edge of the field beyond. Go through a gate and turn right to reach a field corner. Turn left and go along the right edge of two fields. At the corner of the second field, turn right through a gate and go along a faint path halfway up the hill, following a line of small telegraph poles. Cross a barrier stile, and walk along the top edge, looking for a stile on the right. Cross and go diagonally left across a field to reach a road. Cross and go over the stile opposite. Go straight ahead, keeping right of some farm buildings to reach a field with a tower. Now, bear left to reach a swing-gate in the corner. Go through and retrace your steps back to the start.

POINTS OF INTEREST:

Wroxton College – The present house was built by Sir William Pope, on the site of an Augustinian Priory, in 1618. The park was landscaped by Sanderson Miller in 1644. The village church contains monuments to Sir William Pope and his wife.

REFRESHMENTS:

The Blinking Owl Inn, North Newington.
The Roebuck Inn, North Newington.
The North Arms, Wroxton.

Walk 40   COTTISFORD   4¹/₂m (6³/₄km)

Maps: OS Sheets Landranger 152; Pathfinder 1045.

A level walk in an area with some literary interest.

Start: At 579325, the Fox Inn, Juniper Hill.

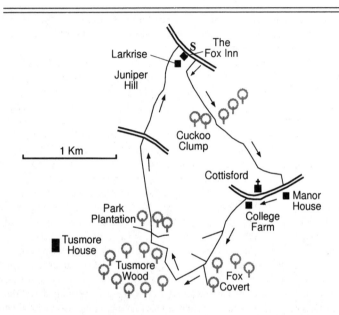

If you use the inn car park, please check with the landlord beforehand. With your back to the inn, turn right along the road. After 150 yards, turn right along a footpath signed ' Cottisford 1'. Go past allotments, on the right, continuing to reach a stile. Cross and bear diagonally left across the field beyond. At the field corner, bear left along a path through woodland. At a path junction, bear right and follow a path along the right edge of a field, with a wood on your right. At the far side, go through a gap in the hedge and continue, now with a small stream between the path and the wood.

At a field corner, turn left, then right, still following the field edge, to reach a road opposite Manor Grange, Cottisford. Turn right along the road, passing Cottisford House and then **St Mary's Church**, both on the right. After a further 120 yards, just past College Farm, on the left, turn left along a farm track. Follow the main track, ignoring a path going off right near a small stream and, at the corner of Fox Covert, a

78

small wood on the left, continue ahead, soon walking with a hedge on your left. At the next cross-tracks, turn right along a field edge, keeping a small plantation on your left. At a path junction, bear right and follow a path around the edge of Tusmore Wood. At the next junction, bear right to reach a T-junction at the edge of a field. Here, turn right and follow a track around the edge of the field. In the distance, to your left, you can just see the buildings of Tusmore House. When the track bends left, turn right towards a gate in a high wire fence.

Do not go through the gate: instead, turn left, keeping the fence on your right. At the fence corner, continue straight ahead to cross a small wooden bridge. Now go up the right edge of a field, walking with a hedge on your right. Over to your left you can see the masts of a radio transmission station. Where a track joins from the left, continue ahead to reach a road. Cross, with care, and continue along a field edge, with the hedge on your left, for 10 yards, then bear left through a gap and continue, but now with the hedge on your right.

At a field corner, bear right, then left around a ditch, and then continue ahead, along the field edge, to emerge, at the far side, on a service road. To see '**Larkrise**', turn right for 130 yards. 'Larkrise' is the white cottage nestling behind 'Queenies', on the right. Retrace your steps and continue along the service road to reach the main road. Turn right to return to the Fox Inn, which will be on your right.

POINTS OF INTEREST:
St Mary's Church, Cottisford – Cottisford was founded during Saxon times, when it was known as *Wolfheysford*. The village was built around the church. During Norman times it was given to the Norman Abbey of Bec. Bec built the present church to replace the earlier Saxon building. It was consecrated, midway through the 13th century, by Grossetete, a scholar Bishop of Lincoln. The writer, Flora Thompson, worshipped here as a child.

Larkrise, Juniper Hill – The actual cottage where Flora Thompson was born has been demolished. The cottage you now see was called End House, but has been renamed Lark Rise Cottage. Flora's family moved here while she was quite young. A plaque on the wall notes that this was where she grew up. Many of the people living in Juniper Hill and Cottisford became characters in the *Larkrise* trilogy. Some of the buildings were renamed. For instance, the Fox Inn became *The Waggon and Horses*. Queenie, who lived at 'Queenie's Cottage', was a bee-keeper and lace-maker.

REFRESHMENTS:
The Fox Inn, Juniper Hill.

Walk 41   PANGBOURNE   4^1/$_2$m (7^1/$_4$km)

Maps: OS Sheets Landranger 175; Pathfinder 1172.

Parts of this walk are beside two rivers, the Pang and the Thames.
There is one gradual ascent up to Pangbourne College.

Start: At 634765, the Village Hall car park, Pangbourne.

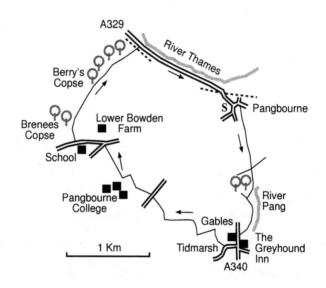

Leave the car park via the pedestrian entrance, near the public conveniences, and turn right. Cross the road, using the crossing and turn right, then left into High Street. At the next junction, go past W H Smith's, on the right, and turn right into The Moors. Follow the private road to its end and go straight on along an enclosed path, with gardens on the left. Go through a swing gate and along the edge of a field, keeping to the right of some small trees. After 40 yards you will reach the River Pang. With the river on your right, go along the bank to reach a concrete footbridge. Cross the bridge and immediately turn left, now walking with the river on the left. Go over a stile and along the left edge of a field. Cross a second stile, to the right of a small stable, and continue ahead to cross a third stile near some gates. After 5 yards, turn left along a gravelled track. Now, about 5 yards after the track bends right, and just before the entrance to a house called 'Longbridge', turn right along an enclosed path, following it as it bends left. Go through a squeeze stile and continue to reach a road (the A340) at Tidmarsh.

Cross the road, with care, and turn left, passing Strachey Close and a gabled house called 'The Gables'. Just opposite the attractive, thatched, 12th-century, Greyhound Inn, on the left, turn right along Tidmarsh Lane. Where the road bends left, turn right through a wooden swing gate. Go along the left edge of a field, through a gate, and along the undulating track beyond. The track meanders left, then right, along the edge of a large field. Just after the track turns right, keep to the left of a hedgerow, going up a slight rise, then turning left along an enclosed path which follows a line of telegraph poles. The path eventually bends right and passes to the right of a house to join a gravelled drive. Continue along the drive to reach a minor road. Cross and go up the track opposite to reach a track junction. Bear right, passing some old garages, on the left, to reach the drive of **Pangbourne College**. Turn right for 30 yards to reach a junction.

Turn sharp left along the road and, after 100 yards, turn right down a drive to reach a road junction. Cross, with care, and turn left up the right-hand fork (signed 'Aldworth 5'). About 20 yards after passing the entrance to a Junior School, on the left, turn right through a swing gate and go along the edge of a field. At the far side, bear right through a gap. Now, bear diagonally left across the next field and, at the far side, go through a gate and along the right edge of a field. At the next field corner, go through a swing gate and continue into Berry's Copse. Follow a meandering path down through the wood and, at the bottom, bear left through a tunnel under a railway to reach the A329. Cross, with care, and turn right along the pavement. The River Thames is now on your left. Follow the A329 back in to **Pangbourne**. About 100 yards after passing under the railway, turn right to return to the car park.

POINTS OF INTEREST:

Pangbourne College – Founded by Sir Thomas Devitt and his son Philip, in 1917, the College educates and trains young people for the Royal and Merchant Navies.
Pangbourne – Neolithic, Roman and Saxon remains have been found in the area. The Roman road from Silchester to Dorchester passed through the parish. Kenneth Grahame, the author of *The Wind in the Willows*, once lived at Church Cottage.

REFRESHMENTS:

The Greyhound Inn, Tidmarsh.
The Swan Inn, Pangbourne.
There are also many other possibilities in Pangbourne.

Walk 42   GORING HEATH $4^{1}/_{2}$m ($7^{1}/_{4}$km)

Maps: OS Sheets Landranger 175; Pathfinder 1172.
A pleasant walk through woodlands near Goring Heath.
Start: At 657791, the Old Post Office, Goring Heath.

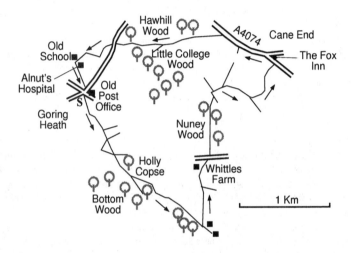

Facing the Old Post Office, take the path to the right of the telephone kiosk. The path soon becomes enclosed by hedgerows. Ignore a path on the right, continuing ahead to reach a tarmac lane. Bear right. passing a house on the right. Go through a gate, and walk along an avenue of trees, passing the aptly-named Rose Cottage on the left. Continue downhill along the winding track to reach Holly Copse Cottage. Take the enclosed path to the right of the cottage, following it downhill, fairly steeply, through the trees.

    Where a path joins from the left, continue ahead for 20 yards, then swing left. After a further 20 yards, fork left along a fairly level path. Follow this meandering path through the woods, and, on emerging, continue ahead along a path enclosed by fences. At the far end of the copse on the right, go past a barrier and, after 25 yards, just before a house, turn left up the right edge of two fields, ascending the second fairly steeply. At the top, look behind for a distant view of Mapledurham House.

Before reaching the field corner, near some stones shaped like the letter H, turn right over a stile, and then turn left along a farm track. Go past Whittles Farm, on the left, and continue to reach a road. Cross and go through a gate just opposite, signed 'Nuney Green $^1/_2$'. Go up the left edge of a field and over a stile at the top. Now, follow a well-defined path through Nuney Wood. Go past some cottages, on the left, to reach a   T-junction. Turn left for 40 yards, then turn right along a bridleway.

At the next path junction, fork right, keeping just inside the edge of a wood. Ignore a track on the left, and continue ahead, with a field on your right. At the next track junction, follow the main track around to the left. When the track ends, carry on along an enclosed path. Enter a field and, after 15 yards, turn left through a gateway. Go along the left edge of a field, then through two gates and a narrow copse to reach a road (the A4074) at Cane End. Turn left, with care, passing the Fox Inn.

Continue along the side of the road, with care, for 700 yards, then, at a right-hand bend, turn left over a stile. Bear slightly right and head along the left edge of a field. Cross a stile in the far corner and continue along a path through Little College Wood. Look for faded white arrow waymarkers on the trees. At a field corner, on the right, turn right for 20 yards, then turn left along a fairly wide track. At the next junction, continue along the main track. Shortly after the track bends right, look for a narrow path on the left.

Veer left along this path, following it downhill to reach a road. Cross and go along the enclosed path opposite. At the far end, cross a stile and bear left along the edge of two fields. In the far corner, turn right along the field edge. Go through a wooden gate and turn left along an enclosed path. Cross a stile and continue between buildings. The plaque on the building on the right notes that the building was once Goring Heath Primary School. Now turn left, passing **Alnut's Hospital**, on the left. After 25 yards, keep to the right of 'The Chaplaincy' sign, and walk ahead over a grass lawn, with a ha-ha on the left. Go along a narrow grass strip to reach a gate on to a road. Opposite is the Old Post Office.

POINTS OF INTEREST:
Alnut's Hospital – In 1724, Henry Alnut left some money in his will for the building of a group of ten almshouses surrounding a chapel, complete with an attractive, white clock tower.

REFRESHMENTS:
The Fox Inn, Cane End.
The Old Post Office, Goring Heath, serves tea and cakes.

Walk 43   CHADLINGTON $4^1/_2$m ($7^1/_4$km)

Maps: OS Sheets Landranger 164; Pathfinder 1068.

A walk through fields to the south of the village of Chadlington, including a short section of the Oxfordshire Way.

Start: At 324225, the Tite Inn, Chadlington.

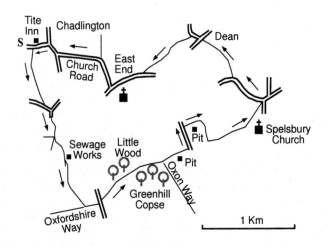

If you use the inn car park, please check with the landlord beforehand. From the inn car park, bear left across the road to the footpath opposite. Follow this clear path, and, at the far field corner, bear right over a small stream. At the top of a short incline, turn left along the left edge of two fields. At the far corner of the second field, go through some bushes to reach a lane. Turn left to reach a road junction. Bear right across the road and go down Brook End opposite, reaching a stile at its far end, by Boot Cottage. Cross and continue along the field edge, walking with a stream on your left. Ignore the first bridge on the left, but, about 40 yards before the far corner, turn left to cross the stream, turning right to walk with the stream on your right. Cross a stile by a ford, go past a sewage works and walk along the right edge of a field. At the far corner, go through a gap and continue along the next field edge to reach a gate in the far corner.

Go through and turn left along the Oxfordshire Way. Cross a road, go through the gate opposite and continue along the right edge of a field. Go through a gate at the far side and turn left along the left edge of the next field. Go past Little Wood, on the left, and, further on, pass Greenhill Copse on the right. Go over a crossing track and ascend to reach a gate. Go through, and continue ahead through some trees. On emerging, go straight on across a field, ignoring the Oxfordshire Way which turns right. Aim to the right of a telegraph pole and pass to the left of some open pit workings to reach a gate on to a lane.

Turn left along the lane for 200 yards, then, just past the entrance to Dean Pit, on the right, turn right through a gate. Follow the left edge of the field beyond, and, at the bottom corner, turn right along the field edge, walking with a hedge on your left. About 20 yards before a grass mound, look for a turning on the left. Go through some bushes and then along an enclosed path, walking with a wooden fence on your right. Cross a stream and go up the left edge of a field. Spelsbury Church can be seen ahead, to the right. At the field corner, turn right and, after 30 yards, turn left along the right edge of a field. Go through a gap in the hedge on the right, and turn left along a track to reach a road. Turn left to reach a road junction. Continue ahead and, where the road bends left, go straight on along a bridleway signed 'Dean $^1/_2$'. Where the main track bends right to a piggery, continue ahead along a path enclosed by hedges. At a path junction, fork left downhill. Cross a bridge over a stream and walk ahead to cross a second bridge. Now, bear left, through a gate, and go up the edge of a field.

Go past a house, on the right, to reach a road. Cross diagonally left, and go up the road opposite. Where the road bends right, turn left through a gate signed 'Chadlington $^1/_2$'. Bear right along the edge of two fields to reach a gate and small stream at the far side of the second field. Go up the left edge of the next field, cross a stile in the top corner and go along a track to reach a road. Turn right through East End. Go past a church, on the left, and, at the next road junction, turn right along Church Road. Follow it around a left-hand bend to reach a T-junction. Turn right and, after 50 yards, turn left, downhill, to return to the Tite Inn, on the right.

POINTS OF INTEREST:
Chadlington – The village is first mentioned in the Doomsday Book as Cedelintone. It is said to be named after St Chad, who once lived in the area. Sir Henry Rawlinson, an expert on Assyria, was born in the Manor House in 1810. He was the owner of *Coronation*, which won the Derby in 1841. The horse was trained at Chadlington.

REFRESHMENTS:
The Tite Inn, Chadlington. Tite is an Oxfordshire name for a small stream.

Walk 44   MINSTER LOVELL $4\frac{1}{2}$m ($7\frac{1}{4}$km)

Maps: OS Sheets Landranger 164; Pathfinder 1091.

A fairly level walk which provides lots of interest, includes visits to the ruins of Minster Lovell Hall and St Kenelm's Church.

Start: At 314110, the White Hart Inn, Minster Lovell.

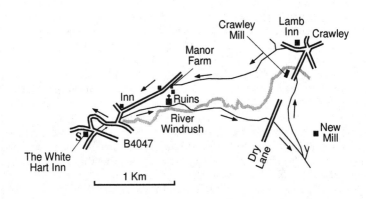

If you use the inn car park, please check with the landlord beforehand. From the inn, cross the B4047, with care, to the bus shelter opposite. Turn right, cross the Leafield road and take the footpath just to the left of a bench seat. Follow this enclosed path down to reach a road. Cross, with care, and turn right. At the road junction, turn left over the River Windrush, then turn right into a sports ground. Now, with the river on your right, walk along the edge of the sports field and, 50 yards before the far end, bear left across the field to reach its far corner. Cross a stile, then bear right to go over a second stile. Walk along the left edge of the field beyond, and, after 150 yards, turn left over a stile and footbridge. Now turn right towards **St Kenelm's Church**. Cross a stile and continue ahead, through the churchyard, passing to the right of the church. The ruins of **Minster Lovell Hall** are on your right. Guide-books are normally available inside the church. Go past the English Heritage kiosk, then bear right to reach and go through a swing gate on the left. To visit the Dovecote, bear left, then return to this point.

From the gate, go straight on, crossing a stile and a plank bridge. Continue ahead, walking with a dry ditch on your right. Maintain direction to reach a bridge over the River Windrush. Cross and bear left, keeping the river on your left. The path joins up with a wider track near a gate: go through and continue ahead. Cross a stile and walk along the right edge of two fields, bearing slightly away from the river. Ignore a stile on the right, continuing to reach a stile in the far corner. Cross this and a second stile, then go ahead along the left edge of the next field. At the far side, ignore a stile on the left, crossing the stile ahead of you. Continue straight on, crossing a stile in the far corner and bearing right along the path beyond, following it as it ascends through a small copse. Go through a gate at the top, and bear right across the field beyond to reach a road (Dry Lane). Cross, with care, and go through the gate opposite.

Bear right across the middle of the field beyond, and, at the far side, go over a stile and turn left towards New Mill. After 10 yards, turn left again, almost doubling back in the direction you have just come. Now follow a narrow path along the field edge. At the far side, go through two gates (ignoring a gate on the left), and walk ahead along a path, with shrubs and hedges on either side, to reach a road. Crawley Mill is just opposite, on the left. Turn right to reach Crawley village green and war memorial.

Turn sharp left up Farm Lane. Where the lane bends right, by Cotswold Cottage, bear left along a signed track. When the track ends, go across a small field to reach a stile. Go over and along the enclosed path beyond. Cross a stile and go along the right edge of a field. At the far side, go through a gate, then bear right across a field to reach a stile in the far right-hand corner. Cross and turn left along a lane. Go past the old Posthouse, on the right, and continue to a road junction. Turn left, cross the river and turn right. After 100 yards, look for steps on your left. Go up these and retrace your outward route back to the start.

POINTS OF INTEREST:

St Kenelm's Church – The church, built in about 1450, is named after a young King of Mercia. Inside is an effigy of William Lovell, who rebuilt the church and the hall.

Minster Lovell Hall – King Richard III and his successor Henry VII stayed at this once fine manor house. The Hall and the Dovecote are in the care of English Heritage.

REFRESHMENTS:

The White Hart Inn, Minster Lovell.
The Lamb Inn, Crawley.

Walk 45   ALDERMASTON WHARF AND VILLAGE $4^{3}/_{4}$m ($7^{3}/_{4}$km)

Maps: OS Sheets Landranger 174 and 175; Pathfinder 1187 and 1188.

A walk with meadows, woods, a village and a canal towpath.

Start: At 601674, Aldermaston Station car park (down side).

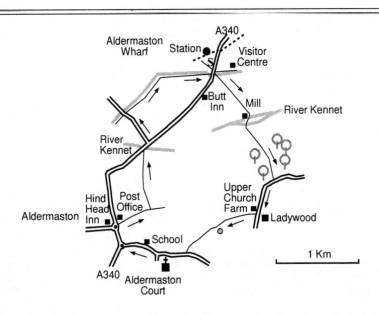

From the car park entrance, cross the road, with care, and go through a swing gate to reach the **Kennet and Avon canal**. Turn left to reach the lift bridge on the A340. Turn right over the bridge, then immediately left and bear right up Mill Lane, passing to the right of Bridge House. Follow the lane to a trout farm on the right and, just past the farm entrance, turn right along a narrow enclosed footpath. The path crosses four footbridges to reach a stile on the far side of the River Kennet. Cross into a meadow, and walk ahead to go through a hedge gap into the next field. Maintain direction, heading just to the right of a telegraph pole, to reach the edge of a wood. Cross a stile and follow a path through Fishers Wood to reach a road. Turn right, passing a saw-mill on the left and Upper Church Farm on the right. At the next house on the left, 'Ladywood', turn right over a stile and go down the right edge of the field to a gate.

Go through a small enclosed area and, at the bottom, turn left over a stile. Turn right, passing a small secluded lake on the left. The path swings left, through trees, to reach a small wooden bridge and stile on the right. Cross and turn right for 15 yards, then turn sharp left across a field, aiming just to the left of four mid-field oaks. At the far side, turn right to reach a stile on the left, near a telegraph pole. Cross and then bear right across a field to a gap near the corner of a small wire fence. Here, bear left and follow the fence to a stile on to a road. Turn right along the road towards Aldermaston, passing the churchyard of **St Mary the Virgin Church**, on the left, and the entrance to Aldermaston Manor, now a large Conference Centre complex. As you continue into **Aldermaston** village look for a high wire fence on the right. This fronts a schoolyard. Next to it is the schoolhouse. On reaching a small village green, with a well in the middle, keep to the right-hand pavement as it swings right to join the A340. Now head downhill, with care, to reach the Hind Head Inn, with its attractive clock and bell tower. Opposite the inn, turn right into Fisherman's Lane, passing to the right of Aldermaston Post Office. Walk along this wide track for 550 yards and, at a footpath sign, turn left along a path which crosses three fields linked by small footbridges. At the far side of the third field cross another footbridge and then bear left, through a small copse, to reach the A340 again. Turn right, with care, cross the River Kennet, and, after about 125 yards, cross, with great care, into Frounds Lane.

Follow the road to the canal bridge, but, just before the bridge, turn right down to the canal towpath and follow it back to Aldermaston Wharf lift bridge. At the bridge (on the A340), turn left over the bridge, then left again to return to the car park.

POINTS OF INTEREST:

Kennet and Avon canal - The British Waterways Visitor Centre, close to the start of the walk, provides information about the canal.

St Mary the Virgin Church – The church dates from the 12th century. On the wall of the south-west buttress there is an early 14th-century scratch nail hole, used as a sun-dial to mark service times. The York Mystery Cycle (which originated in the 14th century) has been staged here for over 30 years.

Aldermaston – John Staid propagated the first William Pear here in 1840. A plaque on the village schoolhouse commemorates the event. Staid is buried in the churchyard.

REFRESHMENTS:
The Butt Inn, Aldermaston Wharf.
The Hind Head, Aldermaston Village.

Maps: OS Sheets Landranger 175; Explorer 3.

A delightful undulating walk through the South Chiltern beech woods, with a chance to visit Grey's Court (in the summer).

Start: At 706834, the Lamb Inn, Satwell.

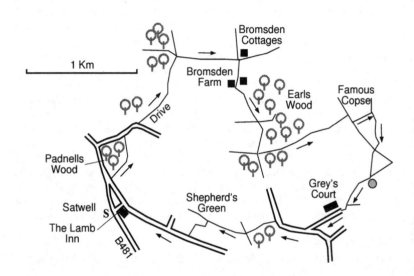

If you use the inn car park, please check with the landlord beforehand. From the inn, cross the road and turn left for 110 yards to reach a road junction. Here, turn right along a narrow path through the woods, continuing ahead at a cross-tracks to reach a road. Turn right, but, after 220 yards, where the road bends sharply right, continue straight ahead along a drive/bridleway signed 'Bix $1^1/_2$'. Follow the drive around a long right-hand bend to reach Bromsden Cottages, on the left at a cross-tracks. Turn right and walk to Bromsden Farm. Go between two barns, then bear right to take a path (signed with a blue arrow) into the woods. After 20 yards, bear left and follow the path as it swings left, then right, descending gradually through the trees. On reaching a cross-tracks continue straight ahead along a broad bridleway, now with a field on your right. At the next cross-track (it is muddy here in wet weather), turn left to ascend a steep path, passing to the left of a National Trust sign stating 'Vermin Control…'. When a wire fence on the right veers away to the right, continue up the hill, following a line of white arrows on the trees. When the path levels out you will see a field over to the right: the path runs about 20 yards in from the field edge, still following the white arrows.

Now, when a fenced corner of a field and a telegraph pole come into view ahead and to the left, look for a tree with a yellow and white cross-tracks marker. Here, turn right (along FP30) and head towards the wood edge, following yellow waymarkers. Cross a stile and go across the field beyond, keeping well to the left of a house on the far side of the field. Cross a stile, a lane, and the stile opposite, then bear left across a field to reach a gap/stile in the hedge opposite. Maintain direction across the next field, crossing a farm track to reach a small wood. Now follow an enclosed path, which bends left, through the wood to reach a gate. Go through, descend a few steps and then turn right, downhill, along a grassy track. Cross a footbridge to the right of a small pond and walk ahead to reach a gate/stile. Beyond, go uphill to reach the next stile. Cross and continue to reach the drive of **Grey's Court** near an entrance kiosk.

Turn right, passing the kiosk and the entrance to the Court, and follow the drive down to a road. Turn right along the road. Ignore the first stile on the left, but, when the road bends right, turn left over a stile and go up the right edge of a field to reach a stile in the top right-hand corner. Cross and continue up through the trees. At the top, cross a stile, going ahead at the next track junction, and, when the trees end, join a path running between a hedgerow and a field. Go over another stile and along a path between wire fences to emerge at a junction of drives at Shepherd's Green. Turn left and walk along the drive to reach a road (look for the telephone box near the road junction). Bear right and follow the road back to **The Lamb Inn** at Satwell.

POINTS OF INTEREST:

Grey's Court – This was once a fortified Manor House. The current gabled brick and flint house is Elizabethan. The garden contains the Archbishop's Maze which is based on a theme of reconciliation. There is also a Tudor donkey-wheel wellhouse. The house and gardens are open to the public during the summer months.

The Lamb Inn – The building has been used as an inn for over 200 years. Originally it was a farm worker's cottage. Dating back to the 16th century, it is one of the oldest buildings in this area.

REFRESHMENTS:

The Lamb Inn, Satwell.

Walk 47　　　**BRADFIELD**　　　$4^3/_4$m ($7^3/_4$km)

Maps: OS Sheets Landranger 174 & 175; Pathfinder 1171 & 1172.

A walk along the Pang Valley to the village of Bradfield and then through the woodlands to the north. It can be muddy during wet weather especially near the River Pang.

Start: At 576715, the Bull Inn, Stanford Dingley.

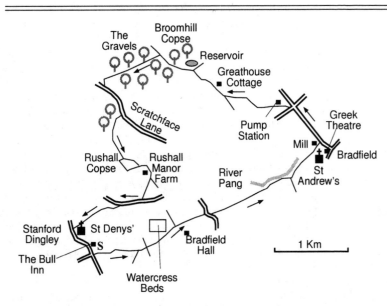

If you use the inn car park, please check with the landlord beforehand. From the inn, turn left along the road to reach a road junction. Turn left along a track, go over a stile and follow the field fence to a swing gate. Go through and along a wide track to reach a stile at the end. Cross and go along the left side of two fields, then through a swing gate and continue along the next field edge, passing some old watercress beds on the left. At a path junction, keep straight on along a wide track. Go through a swing gate and continue with a hedge on your right. Bradfield Hall can be seen to the right here. Maintain direction to reach a road. Turn right for 50 yards, then turn left along the left edge of a field, with a wood on your left. At the far corner of the field, go through a zig-zag stile and walk along the edge of the next field to reach the River Pang.

Go through a squeeze stile and continue along the bank of the River Pang. To the right are the playing fields and buildings of **Bradfield College**. You will soon reach **St Andrew's Church**: join a wide lane and follow it to a road, noting the old mill on the left. Turn left along the road, following it to a crossroads. Cross, with care, and bear left up the steps near a signpost to reach a field corner. Cross the field diagonally right, keeping to the left of an enclosed pumping station, then maintain direction across the next field. After crossing a stile on the far side, turn right along the edge of the next field. At the field corner, turn left for 30 yards, then turn right through a gap. Bear diagonally left across the next field to reach a track (Greathouse Walk). Turn right along the track, passing Greathouse Cottage and a high banked reservoir, both on the right.

Keep to the main track which veers left through Broomhill Copse. After 400 yards the track descends into a dip: about 75 yards up the other side, turn left along a well-defined path through the 'The Gravels'. Continue straight on to reach a stile at a field edge. Cross and turn left along the field edge to reach a stile on to Scratchface Lane. Turn left along the lane and, after 300 yards, turn right along a stony track. Keep to the main track, which bends left, to reach Rushall Copse. Now turn right along a permitted path. The path sweeps left in a wide arc and meets the main track again at a path/track junction. Here, turn right to reach Rushall Manor Farm. Just beyond the last barn on the right, which is worth investigating inside and out, bear right to reach a stile. Cross the field beyond diagonally right to reach a stile on to a road (Back Lane). Turn right and, after 300 yards, turn left along a signed footpath, then immediately right over a stile. Cross a narrow field and, in the next field, keep to the right-hand hedge for 150 yards, then bear left across the field. Cross two further fields to reach St Denys' Church, Stanford Dingley. Go to the right of the church to reach a road and turn left to follow the road back to the Bull Inn.

POINTS OF INTEREST;

Bradfield College – Thomas Stevens, then Lord of the Manor, was instrumental in the founding of Bradfield College in 1842. Over the years the college has grown in size. It is noted for its Greek Theatre.

St Andrew's Church, Bradfield – The original church is 14th-century, but was rebuilt in the 19th century by Gilbert Scott for Thomas Stevens. On the two pillars of the sanctuary at the east end of the church there are stone carvings of a swallow and a sparrow.

REFRESHMENTS:
The Bull Inn, Stanford Dingley.

Walk 48   **BLADON AND BEGBROKE** $4^3/_4$m ($7^3/_4$km)

Maps: OS Sheets Landranger 164; Pathfinder 1092.

A walk from the village where Sir Winston Churchill is buried.

Start: At 448146, the Lamb Inn, Bladon.

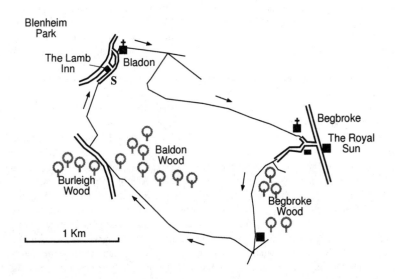

If you use the inn car park, please check with the landlord beforehand. From the rear of the inn, turn left and follow the road around to a road junction. Cross, with care, and bear left up Church Street opposite. At the next junction, bear right, still following Church Street, to reach the lych-gate of **Bladon Church**. Go through the lych-gate and walk to the left of the church. Just after passing the church, look to your right to see the burial place of Sir Winston Churchill and other members of his family. Continue through wrought iron gates and, as you do so, note the plaque on the wall to the right. Turn right up a metalled track and, where the tarmac ends, continue ahead along the, now gravel, then grass, track, with a hedge on your right. At a field corner, turn right and continue, now with a hedge on your left. On reaching a copse on the right, continue ahead along a green lane to reach a gate. Do not go through the gate: instead, turn left across the field, go through a gap and maintain direction across the next field. At the far side, go through a gap, and bear slightly right across the field beyond, heading towards a solitary tree. Go through a gap to the left of a stile, and head towards **Begbroke Church**, with its saddleback roof.

Cross a stile and the field beyond to reach another stile just to the right of the church. Go over and along an enclosed path to reach a gravel drive. Turn left, passing the church, to reach a road, bearing right to reach a T-junction. Turn right up Spring Hill Road, following it to its end where there is a footpath signpost: go straight ahead, following the direction of the fingerpost for 'Cassington $2^1/_4$'. Go through two gates and continue along a farm track, with Begbroke Wood to your left. When you are just past the corner of Begbroke Wood, turn left along a path which crosses a field and then goes along the top edge of the wood. Cross a stile to right of a cattle grid and go along the edge of two fields. In the second field, just past a new house on the left, turn right across the field. At the far side, go through a gap and immediately turn right along the edge of two fields, keeping a hedge and ditch on your right.

At the far corner of the second field, go through a gap and bear right along the field edge. Pass the ruins of an old barn and, at the field corner, turn left for 40 yards, then turn right over a bridge and stile. Continue along the left edge of the field beyond and, at the far corner, turn right. After 10 yards, turn left over a stile and continue, still with a hedge on the left. At the far side, go over a stile and bear left across the field beyond, heading towards the corner of a wood. Here, continue with the wood on your right to reach a stile on to a road. Turn right along the road. Just before the wood on the left ends, turn right over a stile (signed 'Bladon $^1/_4$'). Go along the left edge of a field and, at the far corner, cross a bridged stile and turn left along a field edge. Follow the field edge as it bends right and heads towards houses. At the far corner, cross a stile and walk ahead along a road. Where the road bends right, the Lamb Inn car park will be right in front of you.

POINTS OF INTEREST:

Bladon Church – In 1804 the church was demolished and rebuilt. This was paid for by the Duke of Marlborough. Members of the Churchill family are buried in the churchyard making it a popular tourist attraction.

Begbroke Church – The village of Begbroke is mentioned in the Doomsday Book, where it was valued at 100 shillings. The Norman Church has a saddleback roof, which was added in the 14th century.

REFRESHMENTS:
The Royal Sun, Begbroke.
The Lamb, Bladon.

Walk 49   **LECKHAMPSTEAD**   4³/₄m (7¹/₂km)

Maps: OS Sheets Landranger 174; Pathfinder 1171.

*A fairly level walk across farmland to the south-east of the village
of Chaddleworth, visiting the village of Leckhampstead, with its
interesting clock- faced war memorial.*

Start: At 416773, the Ibex Inn, Chaddleworth.

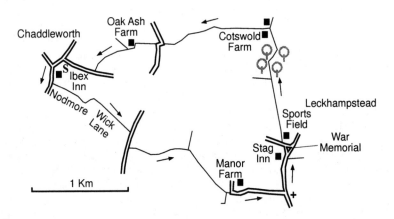

If you use the inn car park, please check with the landlord beforehand. With your
back to the inn, turn left (southwards) to reach a road junction. Bear left along the
Boxford road. As you leave the village, turn left into Nodmore. At the far end, continue
along a bridleway (Wick Lane), following it to reach a road. Turn right and, after
100 yards, turn left across the middle of a field. At the far side, go ahead, walking
with a hedge on your left to reach the field corner. Go through a gap into the next field
and turn.left, then right, following the field boundary.

At the next field corner, at a path junction, bear diagonally right along a fairly
wide path across the middle of two fields. At the far side of the second field, go
through a gap and turn left along a bridleway to reach a farm road (Manor Lane). Go
ahead, passing Manor Farm on the left, to reach a T-junction. There is a church, just
opposite, on the right. Turn left along Shop Lane, passing the Stag Inn on the left, and
continuing to reach the green, with its interesting **War Memorial**.

From the memorial, bear left along a road for 50 yards, then turn right down a track. There is a sports field on the right. When the gravelled track bends left to reach some garages, continue ahead down a grassy track which runs through a pleasant thicket. At the far side of the thicket, turn left along a broad farm track to reach Cotswold Farm, on the left. Now look for a footpath sign on the left. Turn left along this signed path, passing between the farm buildings. Go through a gate on the left and turn right along the farmyard edge to reach a stile in the right-hand corner, just to the right of a barn.

Cross the stile and turn left along the field edge. About 40 yards before the far corner, turn left over a stile, then turn right along a field edge, walking with a hedge on your right. At the far side of the field, continue along a track, between fields, to reach a road. Continue ahead along the road, but, where the road bends left, go straight on through the entrance to Oak Ash Farm, walking along the drive. Just after a left-hand bend there is a pond on the right: take the right-hand fork and follow the drive along an avenue of trees to reach a road. Turn right and follow the road to a T-junction. Turn left to return to the **Ibex Inn**.

POINTS OF INTEREST:

Leckhampstead War Memorial – You will need to look quite closely at this very unusual War Memorial. Comprising an obelisk placed on a plinth, it has two clocks, one facing north, and the other south. It is the clocks which you need to look at, because they have machine gun bullets denoting the minutes, rifle ammunition forming the Roman numerals, and bayonets for hands. The chains surrounding the monument were taken from a battleship which fought at the Battle of Jutland.

The Ibex Inn – The inn is a Grade 3 listed building. During the 17th century the building consisted of two cottages, being part of a larger farm complex. Before becoming an inn, it was an off-licence and, before that, a bakery.

REFRESHMENTS:
The Ibex Inn, Chaddleworth.
The Stag Inn, Leckhampstead.

Walk 50   **NEWBRIDGE** $4^3/_4$m ($7^3/_4$km)
Maps: OS Sheets Landranger 164; Pathfinder 1116.
*A level walk across fields to the village of Northmoor, returning
to Newbridge along the River Thames tow-path.*
Start: At 403014, the Rose Revived Inn, Newbridge.

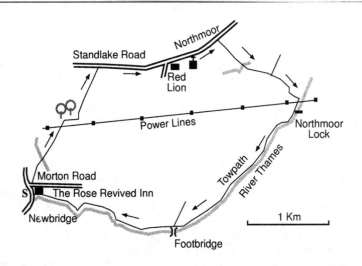

If you use the inn car park, please check with the landlord beforehand. Facing the
Rose Revived Inn, turn left to reach the Moreton Road exit of the car park. Cross the
road to the footpath opposite. Climb over the gate and bear diagonally right across the
field beyond. The path is indistinct, so follow the direction of the fingerpost. At the
far side, cross a wooden bridge and go ahead along a faint track which bends left
under some telegraph wires. About 15 yards before reaching a hedge, bear left and go
through a gap in a hedge, continuing through a narrow band of trees.

   Continue ahead across the next field, aiming just to the left of a pylon. At the far
side, go through a gap in the tree line and walk ahead along a farm track. The track
bends right, then left through a band of trees. When it emerges from the trees, continue
along it to reach a road (Standlake Road). Turn right and follow the road into
Northmoor. Go past the Red Lion Inn, on the right, and, 100 yards further on, the
church, also on the right.

Continue through the village: there is a small path which runs parallel to the road, just to the right of it. About 50 yards beyond the village name sign - on the right, but you only see the back of it - turn right over a stile just to the left of a gate. Go along the gravelled track beyond, following it through several fields. Where the track turns left into the 'R and D A A' member's car park - the sign is on your left - continue straight on along a grassy track. Cross a concrete bridge, go through a gate and across the field beyond to reach the bank of the River Thames.

Turn right along the tow-path, following a delightful section of the Thames back to Newbridge. On the way you will pass Northmoor Lock and, much further on, a footbridge over the Thames. At one time there was a flash weir at this point and a right of way was established across it. When the weir was removed the footbridge was built to replace it.

About 800 yards beyond the footbridge there is a very short detour, near a farm on the right: go through a new wooden swing gate, then a metal swing gate before continuing along the tow-path as it meanders its way to **Newbridge**. Soon the bridge, with its four arches, comes into view. As you approach the bridge you pass through the garden of the Rose Revived Inn: continue across the terrace and then, when you can go no further, turn right to reach the front of the inn and the finish of the walk.

POINTS OF INTEREST:

Northmoor – The village, being low lying, was prone to flooding prior to the Second World War. This changed when a contingent of prisoners of war built a system of drainage ditches in the village. The church dates from the 14th century. One of the tombstones in the churchyard has a reference to the Great Plague in 1665.

Newbridge – The bridge itself does not live up to the name as it is thought to be the second oldest bridge over the Thames. It was built, originally, during the 13th century, and reconstructed during the 15th century. As with Radcot Bridge, the only Thames bridge which is older, Newbridge was involved in numerous skirmishes during the Civil War.

REFRESHMENTS:

The Rose Revived Inn, Newbridge.
The Red Lion, Northmoor.

Walk 51   **LOWER HEYFORD** $4^3/_4$m ($7^3/_4$km)

Maps: OS Sheets Landranger 164; Pathfinder 1069.

An undulating walk, passing close to Rousham House, then crossing fields and going through the village of Steeple Aston before returning beside the Oxford Canal.

Start: At 486248, the Bell Inn, Lower Heyford.

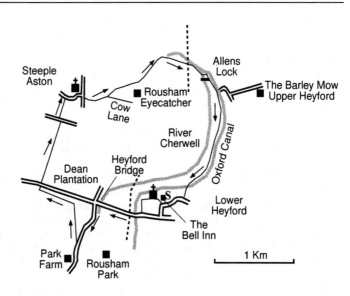

If you use the inn car park, please check with the landlord beforehand. With your back to the inn, turn right along Church Lane. Go past St Mary's Church, then bear slightly left to go through a swing gate partly hidden in the hedge. Follow the enclosed path beyond to emerge just before the Oxford Canal. Turn left and follow the field edge to reach a road (the B4030). Turn right, with care, crossing the canal and a railway line, and continuing to reach the road junction at Heyford Bridge. Here, turn left, walking with the boundary wall of Rousham Park on your left. When the wall ends you will have a fine view of **Rousham House**. Just before Park Farm, on the right, turn right towards the farmyard and go through the first gate on the right. Almost facing the direction you have just come from, aim just to the left of a tree-enclosed

100

pond and continue up the field to reach a stile in the far corner, at the edge of a wood. Go over and turn left along a path which runs just inside the woodland edge. After 550 yards, turn right down a fairly steep bank to reach a road (the B4030 again).

Cross, with care, and go through the gate opposite. Now, with Dean Plantation on your right, follow the field edge down, then up, to reach a stile in the far fence. Go over and bear right along a path which ascends fairly steeply through scrub. At the top, continue across the middle of a field, passing just to the right of a telegraph pole. At the far side, carry on past Seven Springs House, on the right, to reach a road at Steeple Aston. Turn left for 25 yards, then turn right along an enclosed, signed footpath for North Street. Go through a swing gate and down the edge of a field. Pass through a gate at the bottom and then go up a walled path through some trees to reach North Street. The Court House is just opposite. Turn right and follow a twisting road to reach a road junction. The **Church of St Peter and St Paul** is on the left-hand corner. Bear right across the road and go down Cow Lane opposite. At the bottom, look for a gate on the left. Go through the gate and follow a path along the left edge of a field. The **Rousham Eyecatcher** folly will soon be seen on the right.

At the far side, go through a gate in the hedge, then bear left across the middle of a field. Go down a path through scrub, and across a small stream. Now, bear right towards the railway arches. Go under the railway and continue beside the River Cherwell, on the left. Now look for a bridge on the left. Cross this and a second bridge, continuing to reach a bridge over the Oxford Canal. Here, turn right, over a stile, and go down to the tow-path. With the canal on your left and, soon, the River Cherwell on your right, follow the tow-path to reach a drawbridge over the canal. Turn left, over the bridge, and go up the lane to a road junction. Turn right along Freehold Street and, at the next junction, turn right to return to the Bell Inn.

POINTS OF INTEREST:

Rousham House – The house was built for Sir Robert Dormer in 1635. The garden was designed by William Kent who, in 1745, designed Horse Guards Parade in London. The gardens are open daily between 10am to 4.30pm.

Church of St Peter and St Paul – Parts of the church date back to the 12th century. Facing the south porch, the stump of a 15th-century cross can be seen.

Rousham Eyecatcher – The folly, also built by William Kent, is a mock castle gateway with three arches. It can be seen from Rousham House.

REFRESHMENTS:

The Bell Inn, Lower Heyford.
The Barley Mow, Upper Heyford.

Walk 52   **HUNGERFORD**   4³/₄m (7³/₄km)

Maps: OS Sheets Landranger 174; Pathfinder 1186.

A relatively level walk across farmland to the west and south-west of Hungerford, finishing with a short stretch beside the Kennet and Avon Canal.

Start: At 334686, the Church of St Lawrence, Hungerford.

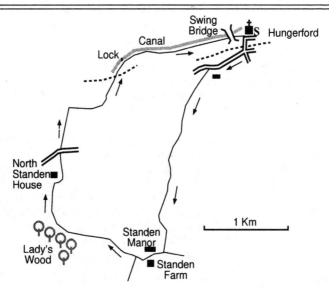

With your back to the main entrance of the church, turn right along the road. Follow the road as it bends left and goes under a railway to reach a T-junction. Turn right along Smithan Bridge Road. About 50 yards after passing Hungerford Trading Estate, on the left, turn left through a gate and follow a path across two fields. At a hedge corner in the second field, continue ahead, walking with a hedge on your left, and, just before reaching the far corner, bear right to reach a stile in the hedge.

    Cross the stile and walk ahead, going over a track and through a young plantation to reach a stile at the far side. Cross and, after 10 yards, ignore a stile on the left and bear right through a gap. Turn left along the edge of a field, walking with a hedge on your left. At the far corner of a very large field, go over a stile and maintain direction across the next field to reach a stile at the far side. Cross and turn right along a lane.

Do not go through the gates of Standen Manor: instead, follow the lane towards Manor Farm. Go past some barns on the left, then, where the main lane turns left, continue ahead along a gravelled track. Keep to the left of some barns, then, when the gravelled surface ends, continue ahead on a track along the left edge of a field. At the far corner, go through a gap and walk along the edge of a wood. The wood is on your left and there are telegraph lines overhead.

At a fence corner on the right, bear right across a field, going under the telegraph wires. At the far side, turn right along a faint track, keeping a wood on your left. At the field corner, bear left through a gap and go ahead along a track which bends right, then left, to pass to the right of North Standen House. Join the main drive of the house and follow it to a road. Cross the road, with care, and go along the track opposite to reach a track junction.

Turn right and follow a track, bearing left with it to go through a gap at the far corner of the field. Now, where the main track bears right, uphill, turn left to go down the left edge of a field, walking with a fence on your left. After 300 yards, look for a stile on your left: the hedge is sometimes overgrown and it is quite easy to walk past this stile. Go over and turn right along a narrow enclosed path. Go up some steps and cross the railway line, taking great care.

Go down the steps on the other side, over a stile, and bear right along the left edge of a field, heading towards some houses. Cross a stile and, after 5 yards, turn right along the canal tow-path. Now, with the canal on your left, follow the tow-path back to **Hungerford Church**. At the swing bridge just before the church, bear right through the churchyard, passing to the right of the church to regain the start.

POINTS OF INTEREST:

The Church of St Lawrence, Hungerford – Built in 1816, the church was constructed of Bath stone, which had never been used in the town previously. It was built on the site of a 13th-century church which had become so dilapidated that it had to be demolished. There are some relics from the original church, one being a memorial to a knight.

REFRESHMENTS:

The Bear Inn, Hungerford. This 15th-century inn, situated on the Bath Road, was used as the venue, in 1688, for a meeting between representatives of James II and William of Orange, which resulted in the end of the reign of the House of Stuart. There are also several other inns in Hungerford.

Walk 53   NORTH LEIGH ROMAN VILLA   5m (8km)

Maps: OS Sheets Landranger 164; Pathfinder 1091.

A walk back in time visiting a Saxon church and the ruins of an old Roman villa.

Start: At 399144, the Leather Bottel Inn.

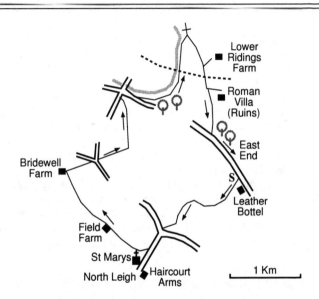

If you use the inn car park, please check with the landlord beforehand. From the inn, turn left (north-west) along the road and, after 30 yards, turn left between houses to go along a signed footpath for North Leigh. Go through two gates then bear left across a field to its far corner. Cross a stile and bridge and bear right across the next field, heading towards the rightmost of four trees. At the field corner, go through a gap into the field on the left and turn right to walk along the right edge of two fields.

At the far corner of the second field, go through a gate and down a path enclosed by hedges. When the hedge on the right ends, you will be able to see **North Leigh Church** ahead of you: the path now veers right, downhill, to a gate and road. Cross the road, with care, and head up the road opposite. After 300 yards, just before the church, turn right along the track to Field Farm. Do not go through the gate into the farmyard: instead, go through the gate just to the right of it. Keep the farmyard fence on your left and follow to reach a gate in the field corner. Go through and head straight across the field, aiming just to the left of a hedge coming up from the right. Continue ahead, with the hedge on your right, towards Bridewell Farm. The path goes through a gap into the farmyard.

Head towards the large barn, but just before reaching it, turn sharp right and follow a path diagonally across the field, heading away from the barn, to reach a footbridge. Cross and bear right across the next field to reach a road. Turn right to a road junction. Turn left to the upper road and the gate opposite. Go through the gate and continue ahead along the right edge of the field beyond. The path descends gradually in to a small valley: when the hedge on the right ends, go straight on across a narrow strip of field and through a gap to reach a crossing track.

Turn left and follow the track, with a small ditch on your right, to reach a road. Turn right to a crossroads, then right again for 20 yards to take a path on the left. Soon you reach the bank of the River Evenlode: continue ahead through trees, with the river on your left and a steep woody bank on the right. Go under the railway and walk for a further 400 yards to where the path veers right to reach a gate on the left. Now turn right up a farm track, heading away from the gate. After 500 yards a track to Lower Ridings Farm joins from the left. Continue straight ahead, over the railway bridge, and, after a further 200 yards, turn left down a track to visit the **North Leigh Roman Villa**. Retrace your steps and turn left to reach a road. Turn left and continue through East End village and back to the Leather Bottel Inn, on the right. The open fronted gardens are quite colourful and interesting.

POINTS OF INTEREST:
St Mary's Church, North Leigh – This is a Saxon church, originally built around 1040. The Normans added a new nave in about 1165. The bowl of the Norman font was re-chiselled in 1842 after being used as a water butt. The pride of the church is the exquisitely stone carved Wilcote Chapel, built in 1442 in commemoration of Sir William Wilcote.

North Leigh Roman Villa – The villa is thought to have been a civilised country house, situated not far from the Roman road known as Akeman Street. The floor and foundations of two wings, dating back to the 1st to 4th century, are exposed. A mosaic floor has been covered over, but is viewable.

REFRESHMENTS:
The Leather Bottel, East End.
The Harcourt Arms, North Leigh.

Walk 54   PISHILL   5m (8km)

Maps: OS Sheets Landranger 175; Explorer 3.

A pleasant walk in the Chiltern hills, through woods and farmland. There are a number of steep ascents and descents.
Start: At 720888, on Russell's Water Common. Park with care on the grass verge.

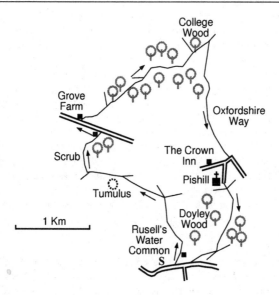

Walk down the road towards Stonor and turn left along the track signed for Maidensgrove Farm. Cross the farmyard, keeping to the left of the farmhouse, and go over the stile opposite. Follow a fenced path through a paddock, cross another stile and continue along a path which descends steeply, through woodland, to the valley bottom. Continue up the other side on a track, passing through **Doyley Wood**, to reach a field. Bear left around the field edge and, on reaching the edge of a wood, turn left along a track just inside the wood edge. Go over a farm track and continue ahead towards some farm buildings. Just past the farm buildings, on the left, there is a large Bronze Age tumulus amongst the trees. Go through a gate and along a wide track across the common, with good views to the left. On reaching scrubland, turn right and follow a path along the left edge of the common for 500 yards to reach the common's far corner. Now turn left into the wood. Follow the path as it swings right and descends through the wood to reach a road, at Glade House. Turn left along the road for 500 yards to reach a pair of tall iron gates on the right, signed for Grove Farm. Turn right through the gates and follow the track around to the right. After 10 yards, veer left along a path, ascending steeply through Shambridge Wood.

Follow the direction of the white arrow waymarkers on the trees, ignoring paths to the left, to reach a path junction. Keep straight on along the path, which bears right, descends, and then ascends to the top of the hill. At a junction of paths, turn right and, after 10 yards, bear left, downhill. At the bottom, cross a track and continue straight ahead along a path which ascends steeply through an open area. When track bends left, go straight ahead along a path which bends right into a plantation. Continue along a well-defined path to reach an open area. Cross diagonally to the left and take a narrow path which climbs steeply uphill to reach a cross-tracks at the top. Do not turn left to reach a stile: instead, turn right and follow the Oxfordshire Way. In the valley bottom, at the edge of a wood, cross a stile and turn left to follow a track to the road at **Pishill**. Turn right along the road for 40 yards, then turn left, uphill, to Pishill Church.

Walk past the church and, at the top of the rise, go straight ahead, still following the Oxfordshire Way signs. Go through a gap and follow a field edge downhill, then uphill to enter Pishillbury Wood. The path ascends steeply through the wood: at the top keep straight on, with a field on your right, to reach a path junction. Bear right, up a bank, towards houses to reach a gravel track, and follow the track to a road. Turn right and follow the road back to the start.

POINTS OF INTEREST:

Doyley Wood – The wood is named after the D'Oilly family who lived in the manor of Pishill Napper during the Middle Ages. An important family, they owned land throughout Oxfordshire.

Pishill – It is thought that the origin of the village's name is *'the hill where peas grow'*. Pishill Church was originally built during the 12th century, but was rebuilt, by the Rev Keene of Swyncombe, in 1854.

REFRESHMENTS:

The Crown Inn, Pishill.

Walk 55   **STONOR PARK**   5m (8km)

Maps: OS Sheets Landranger 175; Explorer 3.

A pleasant walk in the Chiltern hills, through woods and a deer park, with the added bonus of a visit to Stonor House.

Start: At 720888, on Russell's Water Common. Park with care on the grass verge.

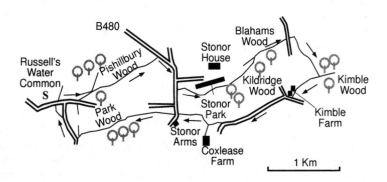

Follow the road towards **Stonor**, going past the track leading to Maidensgrove Farm and continuing down the hill for 250 yards. At the Oxfordshire Way sign, turn left along a path into the wood. At the first path junction, continue straight ahead, following the white arrow waymarkers. At the next path junction, bear right through Pishillbury Wood. The path, fairly level at first, soon starts to descend and you may catch your first sight of Stonor Park and House ahead. The path leaves the wood and descends to reach a road (the B480). Turn right, with care, towards Stonor village. Go past the main entrance to **Stonor House**, on the left, and, after a further 150 yards, turn left, through an iron kissing gate into the grounds of Stonor Park. There is a sign 'Southend $1^1/_2$'.

    Follow the path, which ascends fairly steeply at first, with excellent views of the Chiltern Hills to the left, and of Stonor House itself. The path continues through the deer park - where deer may also be seen - ascending gradually to reach a gate in the boundary fence. Go through and continue along a narrow path through the trees. The path bends left to meet a wider cross-track: turn right and ascend, fairly steeply, through Kildridge Wood.

At the top, when a field edge is reached on the left, continue straight ahead to reach a road. Cross the road, with care, and continue along the track opposite. At its end, go over a stile and follow the right edge of the field beyond to reach a stile in the far right-hand corner. Do not cross the stile in right-hand fence: instead, cross the stile in the corner and follow the path beyond down through woodland to meet a wide cross-track in the valley bottom. Turn right and follow the track to reach a road at Kimble Farm. Turn right and walk to a road junction. Go straight ahead, with good views to the left. When the road bends sharply left, continue straight ahead along the farm track leading to Coxlease Farm. The high fence of Stonor Park will be on your right. When the farm track bends left towards the farm buildings, go straight ahead along a path beside the park fence. The path bends right, then left, as it descends, steeply, to reach the road (the B480) in Stonor village.

Cross, with care, and turn left. After 20 yards, just past Well Cottage on the right, turn right up a narrow enclosed path. Cross a stile and head uphill across two fields, passing just to the right of a copse to reach a stile at the edge of Park Wood. The path continues to ascend, gradually, through the wood to reach a stile at the far side. Go over and head across a field towards some houses. At the far side of the field, bear left along a track between cottages to reach a drive. Turn right and, ignoring all turns to both left and right, continue to reach Russell's Water Common. Now bear right across the Common to return to the start.

POINTS OF INTEREST:

Stonor – In a charter of the Mercian King Offa, dated AD774, Stonor appears as Stanora Lege, meaning *stony hill*.

Stonor House – The first recorded building is believed to date from the late 12th century. The first additions occurred between 1280 and 1331. Brick was first used during the early 15th century. The house has remained in the Stonor family since it was first built. The house is usually open to the public between April and September. There is a gift shop and a tea room.

REFRESHMENTS:

The Stonor Arms, Stonor.
The Tea Room at Stonor House.

Maps: OS Sheets Landranger 174; Pathfinder 1187.

A walk in the River Enborne Valley, passing two interesting churches. It also includes a route through Wasing Park. There are no hills on this walk.

Start: At 557647, St Peter's Church, Brimpton.

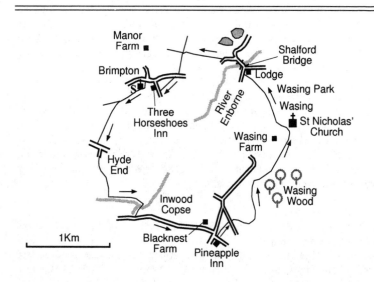

Facing St Peter's Church, **Brimpton**, take the walled path to the left of the churchyard. Then, with a hedge on your right, go straight ahead for 300 yards before bearing left along a grass strip path. The path passes between paddocks to reach a road. Turn left and, soon, take the right branch at a fork. The road soon becomes gravelled and you pass Hyde End House on the left: when the track swings left, cross the stile ahead. Go across the field beyond to reach the bank of the River Enborne: turn left along the river-bank. Near the end of the second field, turn right over a footbridge and follow a path which runs through the edge of Inwood Copse to reach a lane. Turn left along the lane for just over ¹/₂ mile to reach a cross-roads. Here, cross, with care, and turn right, then left along the B3051 to reach the Pineapple Inn, on the right. Opposite the inn, turn left along a path through some paddocks to reach another road.

Cross the road, with care, and continue along a byway. Follow the main track, bending right, then reaching a left bend. Here, go straight on along a footpath, keeping a wood to your right, to reach a T-junction. Turn left along the wood edge, following a permitted path. Where a right of way joins from the left, carry straight on, following a line of yew trees. The path becomes hedged, then fenced, as you walk through Wasing Park and ahead you can see Wasing House. Cross a broad crossing track and go straight on through a squeeze stile to reach a drive and **St Nicholas' Church**, just the other side. Turn left along the drive, following it to reach a lodge and a road. Here, turn left, then right across Shalford Bridge over the River Enborne. At the next road junction, take the left-hand fork and, after 200 yards, where the road bends left, go straight ahead, passing to the left of a metal gate, to follow a footpath. There are gravel working ponds on the right here.

At the far end of the large open field on the right, turn left along an enclosed path to reach a road at Glebe Cottage. Turn right for 25 yards, then turn left through a swing gate. Half-way up the left side of the field, go over a stile and maintain direction to reach the far side of a field. Here, go along a narrow path, between houses, to reach a housing estate road. Follow the road through the estate to reach a T-junction. Cross, with care, to reach the entrance to the almshouses on the other side. Now turn right along the pavement, following it past the Three Horseshoes Inn to reach the war memorial. Here, turn left along a drive to return to St Peter's Church.

POINTS OF INTEREST:

Brimpton – St Peter's Church is a landmark which can be seen from miles around. It was built in about 1870, but in 14th century style, by the architect John Johnson. In the grounds of Manor Farm, just north of the village, is the 14th century Knights Templars' Chapel of St Leonard.

St Nicholas' Church, Wasing – The church, set in the middle of a park, began as a small medieval building with a short nave and chancel. In the 18th century the nave was extended and the south transept added. Wasing Place, near the church, was built during the 1770s. It was rebuilt, using old materials, after it was burnt down during the Second World War.

REFRESHMENTS:

The Three Horseshoes Inn, Brimpton.
The Pineapple Inn, Brimpton Common.

Maps: OS Sheets Landranger 164; Pathfinder 1092.

*A fairly level walk in the grounds of Blenheim Palace, through
parkland much of which was landscaped by Capability Brown.*
Start: At 447168, the Hensington Road car park, Woodstock.

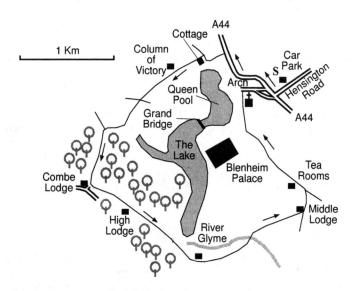

Go through the main entrance of the car park and turn right along Hensington Road to
reach the A44. Turn right, then left, crossing the road via the zebra crossing. Turn
right along the pavement and follow the A44 as it bends left downhill. As you ascend
the other side of the dip, look for a small church on the right. Here, turn left along a
short road, and then go through a swing gate into Blenheim Park. Bear left along a
track, which descends towards the lake, to join a metalled track. Follow this track
around, passing a cottage on the left. A few yards further on, at a path junction, turn
sharp left, still keeping the cottage to your left. Just before you arrive opposite the
cottage, veer right up a grassy bank and go through a clump of trees. Now head for the
Column of Victory, which is clearly seen ahead. From the column look left for a good
view of **Blenheim Palace**.

Bear left to reach a fence corner, then maintain direction, keeping the fence to your right. When the fence ends, go straight on to reach a drive. Cross and follow a path down through trees. At the bottom, at a path junction, turn right and head for a stile in the fence. Cross and turn right along a faint track which bends left between two tree-topped mounds to reach a tarmac drive. Continue ahead up the drive, following it to reach Coombe Gate on the right. Do not turn right through the gate: instead, continue ahead along the drive, which cuts through some ancient woodland. Go past a turning and a pond, on the right, continuing ahead to reach a lodge on the left. Here, carry straight on, soon with an open field on your right. Soon, the River Glyme comes into view on the left. The drive crosses an attractive stone bridge and, beyond, bends right. Look left here for another fine view of Blenheim Palace. On reaching a drive junction, at Middle Lodge, continue straight on, crossing a cattle grid, to reach the next drive junction.

Turn left, passing a refreshment area and a miniature railway on the left. Continue along the drive to reach another junction. On your left now you will have your closest view of Blenheim Palace. Go straight over the crossing drive, heading towards the Woodstock Arch entrance in the distance. On your left you will see the lake and the Grand Bridge. Go through the arch and bear right along Park Street, passing a tearoom on your right. A little further on there are some old stocks on the left. At the Municipal Building, fork right and follow the left-hand pavement which, at the far end, bends left through a short alley to reach the A44 near a telephone box. Cross the road, via the zebra crossing, and turn right for 10 yards. Now turn left into Hensington Road following it for 200 yards before turning left back into the car park.

POINTS OF INTEREST:
Blenheim Palace – Henry I originally built a Manor House here during the 12th century. Since then houses on the site have been the birthplace of, amongst others, Edward, the Black Prince, and Sir Winston Churchill. In 1504 Elizabeth I was imprisoned here. During the early 1700s, the house was presented to John Churchill, the 1st Duke of Marlborough, by Queen Anne in gratitude for his victory at Blenheim in Bavaria. Badly damaged during the Civil War, the former Manor House was demolished and a new Palace was built. The Park was later landscaped by Capability Brown. It is open to the public.

REFRESHMENTS:
There are a number of places in Woodstock and a tearoom in the Park.

Walk 58　　　　　　　　HETHE　　　　　　　5m (8km)

Maps: OS Sheets Landranger 164; Pathfinder 1069 and 1070.

From the attractive village of Hethe, this fairly level walk crosses farm fields to the little village of Stoke Lyne.

Start: At 594295, Hethe War Memorial.

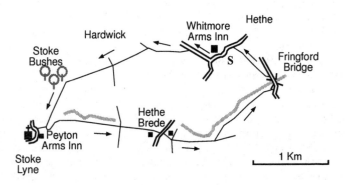

Facing the attractive, thatched, Manor Farm House, just opposite the memorial, turn left along the road, passing **Hethe Church** and the Whitmore Arms, both on the right. At the road junction, bear right and, about 100 yards after passing the last house on the right, turn left along a track which passes to the left of some allotments. At the far end of the allotments, continue ahead along an enclosed path. When a wooden fence, on the right ends, carry straight on along the edge of a field. At the field corner, near a lone tree, go straight across the middle of the next field. Cross a farm track, go through a gap in the hedge, and bear diagonally left across the next field. In the far left-hand corner, go through another gap and walk along the right edge of the field beyond. The village of Hardwick can be seen over to your right. At the far corner, continue ahead through a small copse, then go along the right edge of a field to reach a gate. Go through and ahead along the field boundary.

Cross a wide farm track, noting the tap which stands almost in the middle of the track junction. Continue ahead, keeping to the left of a hedge. At the next field corner, go directly ahead across a field aiming for the near left corner of Stoke Bushes Wood. Here, go through a gap and bear left across the next field, heading away from the wood. In the opposite corner, go through a gate and cross a small stream. Now, head towards the houses of **Stoke Lyne**. Go through a second gate, then ahead up a gravelled road, bending right to reach a road junction. Turn left up the road, passing the Peyton Arms Inn, on the left, to reach Stoke Lyne Church, on the right. Leave the church and turn left, retracing your steps to the Peyton Arms. Just past the inn, turn right along an enclosed path between houses. Go over a stile and cross the middle of the field beyond. At the far side, turn left, along the field edge.

At the far corner, go through a gate and bear left along the left edge of the next field, soon being joined by a small stream on the left. Go over a crossing path and continue to a gate. Go through and along the field boundary, heading towards a distant house. Go through another gate, to the right of a telegraph pole, and along the left edge of the next field. At a house called Hethe Brede, turn right for 30 yards, then left to reach a road. Cross, and continue ahead, passing to the right of two barns, and then going through two farm gates.

Bear left across the middle of a field, and, in the next field, aim to the left of a lone tree. At the far side, go through a gap and walk ahead for 50 yards, then veer left along a path, following it across three fields, with two footbridges between them, to reach the bank of a stream. Here, turn right and follow the stream to reach a road. Turn left and follow the road over a bridge. After another 30 yards, turn left through a gate, then bear right up the edge of a field. Cross a stile and walk ahead for 150 yards, then cross a stile in the right-hand fence and turn left along the field edge. Go past a sewage works, on the left, and continue down the field, passing some houses, to reach a road. Turn left and follow the road back to the War Memorial.

POINTS OF INTEREST:

Hethe Church – Originally built in the 14th century, Hethe Church was rebuilt by the well-known architect, George Street, in 1859.

Stoke Lyne – The village has no village hall so, the Peyton Arms is used as a meeting place. The Rev William Bryant MA, one time vicar of St Peter's Church, used to walk round the church tower calling the parishioners to worship.

REFRESHMENTS:

The Whitmore Arms, Hethe.
The Peyton Arms Inn, Stoke Lyne.

Walk 59   STANFORD IN THE VALE   5m (8km)

Maps: OS Sheets Landranger 164; Pathfinder 1135.

A pleasant walk in the lovely Vale of the White Horse.

Start: At 339930, the Horse and Jockey Inn, Stanford in the Vale.

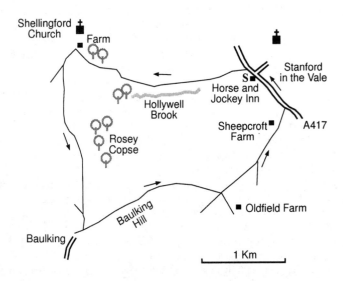

If you use the inn car park, please check with the landlord beforehand. Facing the inn, go along the drive to its right and, at the ornamental entrance to a house, bear right to continue along an enclosed path. Follow the path to a stile. Go over and across the middle of the field beyond. Look left here for a distant view of White Horse Hill. Go through a gate and along the left edge of a field and, at the far side, cross a gate stile and walk ahead to reach the field corner. Turn right and, after 20 yards, turn left across a small bridge with a stile each end. Cross the middle of the next field, go over a small bridge, and bear diagonally right across the next field. In the far right-hand corner, cross a bridge and stile, and turn left before bearing right across the middle of the field, aiming for a stile 50 yards to the right of a small copse. Go over the stile, cross a track, and go over the stile opposite. Now bear right to reach a stile in the right-hand fence. Continue across the next field to reach a bridge near a corner of

Fishpond Copse. Cross the bridge, and take a narrow path into the copse. After 10 yards, turn left through a gate. Turn right, and then bear slightly left across the corner of a field to reach a farm gate. Go through and, after 20 yards, turn left over a fence. Now bear right to reach a stile in the fence ahead, near a footpath sign. To your right you can see the steeple of **Shellingford Church**.

Cross the stile and turn left along a farm track. After 200 yards, turn left through a gate. Bear right across the field beyond to reach a gap in a line of trees. Go through a gate, then bear diagonally left across a field and go over a stile at the far side. Bear left across the next field to reach a stile between two gates, just to the right of a willow tree. Continue ahead, keeping a fence on your right. Rosey Copse is on the left. In the far corner, turn right over the small River Ock. Turn left across the middle of a field, keeping to the right of a tree in the centre. Go through a gap and ahead along the edge of the next field. At the far side, turn right for 30 yards, then turn left through a gap to reach a green gate. Go through and along the left edge of a small field. The village of **Baulking** is on your right. In the far corner, go through a gate and follow a bridleway over Baulking Hill, descending to reach a gate. Go through and cross the next field.

Cross a small bridge and bear slightly right across a field, heading towards Oldfield Farm. At the far side of the field, go through a gap and cross a bridge. Immediately turn left along a field edge, walking with a ditch on your left. Go over a crossing track and, in the corner, cross a bridge and stile. Bear slightly left across the next field. Cross a stile and swing left towards Sheepcroft Farm. Just before the farm, turn right over a stile. Now, keep the farm on your left and bear left across the field to reach a stile in the far left-hand corner. Cross the stile and turn left, with care, along the road (the A417), following it back to the Horse and Jockey Inn, on the left.

POINTS OF INTEREST:

Shellingford Church – John Morton, one of the rectors of this part-Norman, 12th-century church, went on to become Archbishop of Canterbury and Chancellor of England during the reign of Henry VII.

Baulking – The village, once in Berkshire, has a large goose green, and retains much of the character of a typical old English village. During the 1920s point-to-point races were held on Baulking Hill.

REFRESHMENTS:

The Horse and Jockey Inn, Stanford in the Vale.

Maps: OS Sheets Landranger 163 and 164; Pathfinder 1068.

*A pleasant walk along lanes and tracks, providing good views
of the surrounding countryside.*

Start: At 282241, the Chequers Inn, Churchill.

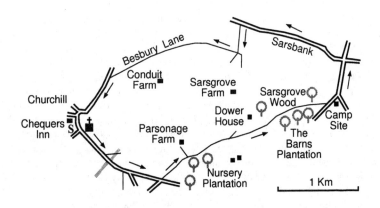

With your back to the inn, turn right to reach a road junction, with **All Saints' Church**
on the left. Carry straight on down Church Road. Ignore a footpath on the left and
continue over Sars Brook and up the other side. At the next road junction, continue
straight ahead towards Chadlington. After 450 yards, at a road junction, turn left
along a 'No Through Road'. There are good views of rolling countryside and back
towards Churchill from here. Go past a track to Parsonage Farm, on the left, and a
plantation, on the right, continuing ahead to pass through a gateway. Just beyond, on
the left, is the drive to Dower House.

Carry on along the track, now walking with a stone wall on your right and Sarsgrove Wood on your left. The track passes through the Barns Plantation and continues to reach a gate on to a road (the A361). Turn left down the road, keeping to the grass verge and taking great care as the A361 can be busy. Go past a road junction, on the right, and continue to the next cross-roads.

Turn left towards Cornwell. Follow the road for approximately $^3/_4$ mile, then, just before a track, on the left, leading to Sarsgrove Farm, turn left over a stile. Bear right across the corner of a field to reach a stile in the right-hand fence. Go over on to the lane. When the book was being prepared, a new wall was being built where you leave the road to go into the field requiring walkers to continue to the lane and to turn left along it. Now, where the lane bends left, turn sharp right along a farm track. There are some good views of Churchill and its church ahead, to the left, from here.

Now, ignore a turning on the left to Conduit Farm, continuing ahead to go through a gate. Beyond the gate the track becomes metalled (Besbury Lane): follow the lane down to a road. Turn left and follow the road back into **Churchill**: the Chequers Inn will be on the right.

POINTS OF INTEREST:

All Saints' Church – The magnificent tower of the church is a replica of Magdalen in Oxford. The walls and ceiling are based on New College and Christ Church Hall, also in Oxford. The church was designed by Squire Langston and built in 1826. It is a much loved local landmark which can be seen for miles, as you can tell from this walk.

Churchill – The village has an impressive history. Warren Hastings was born here in 1732. At the age of 17 he set sail for India. In 1773 he became the first Governor General of India. Then, in 1769, William Smith, the 'Father of British Geology', was born in Churchill. The Smith Memorial stands centrally in the village.

REFRESHMENTS:
The Chequers Inn, Churchill.

HENLEY-ON-THAMES 5m (8km)

Maps: OS Sheets Landranger 175; Explorer 3.

An undulating walk from the town renowned for its annual regatta. Providing good views in places, the route also takes you through a bluebell wood.

Start: At 763826, Henley Bridge.

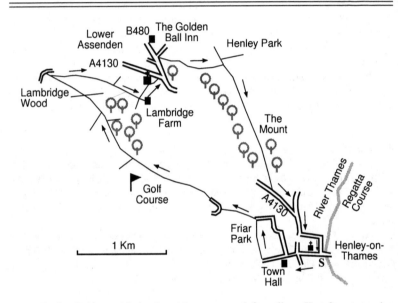

From Henley Bridge, with the Angel Inn, on your left, walk up Hart Street, passing St Mary's Church and an interesting Victorian water fountain, on your right. Opposite the church, on the other side of the road, is the Speaker's House, marked by a plaque. Continuing up Hart Street, you will pass Blandy's House, also on the right. At the traffic lights, continue straight ahead up West Street, passing to the right of the Town Hall. At a road called Hop Gardens, turn right. Go past Badgemoor School, on the left, then turn left up Crisp Road. Now look for a footpath sign on the left, and follow the path, enclosed between fences to reach a minor road. Turn right, go past Lambridge House and through a gate, or over the stile just to the left of it. Where the track beyond bends right, go straight ahead over a stile and follow a track across Badgemoor Golf

Course. Where the main track bends left, continue ahead, walking with trees on your left, to reach the edge of Lambridge Wood. Go over a stile, and walk into the wood, following the direction of the yellow waymark arrows on the trees. Ignoring all turns to the left and right, continue straight on, following path No. 48 through the wood to reach a road. Turn sharp right along a track, almost doubling back in the direction you have just come. Follow the track to reach, and pass, Lambridge Wood House, then continue ahead for another 400 yards to reach a path junction. Turn left and follow a path, which becomes enclosed, down to reach the A4130. There is a small church and cemetery on your left.

Turn right, with care, along the A4130 for 50 yards to reach a road junction. Now cross, with care, and turn left along the B480, heading towards Lower Assendon. Go past a turning on the left, and, at the next junction, bear right. After 30 yards, turn right along a waymarked lane. Go through a gate and continue along a track. The track ascends quite steeply to Henley Park. Ignore a path which bends to the left and continue ahead to reach a cross-tracks at the top of a fairly wide plateau. Here, turn right along the Oxfordshire Way. Level at first, the path soon starts a gradual descent. There are some good views of the valleys either side from here. As you descend, look out for an ancient earthwork mound, on your right, known as The Mount. Shortly after passing The Mount you will reach a gate at the edge of woodland: go through the gate and follow the path beyond, which descends, fairly steeply in parts, through the wood. Near the bottom woodland edge, the path veers right to leave the wood. Continue along the enclosed path to reach the A4130. Turn left, with care, towards **Henley-on-Thames**. At the road junction, cross and follow the road around to the right. After 250 yards, turn left. Go past the Kenton Theatre, on the left, and Henley Brewery, on the right. Just before the road turns right, beside the river, turn right along a narrow alley. The alley passes some very interesting almshouses to emerge at St Mary's Church. Turn left to return to Henley Bridge.

POINTS OF INTEREST:
Henley-on-Thames – The town is the home of the famous Henley Regatta, and has much of great historical interest. The Town Hall was built, in 1796, on the site of a medieval Guildhall. St Mary's Church and Almshouses date back to the 14th and 15th centuries; while Henley Brewery dates from 1799. Henley Bridge was built in 1786 to replace a wooden bridge swept away by a flood in 1774.

REFRESHMENTS:
There are numerous opportunities in Henley.

Walks 62 & 63   **ALDWORTH**   5m (8km)
or $6^1/_2$m ($10^1/_2$km)

Maps: OS Sheets Landranger 174; Pathfinder 1171 and 1155.
A chance to visit the local church to see the famous 'Aldworth giants', and a walk along an ancient track.
Start: At 555796, the Bell Inn, Aldworth.

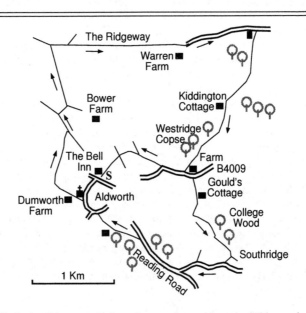

There is limited parking near the inn: please park considerately. With your back to the inn, go down the road opposite, noting the old village well of **Aldworth** on the left. After 300 yards you will reach **St Mary's Church**, on the right. As you pass the church, note the old water pump on the bank of the churchyard. At the corner of the churchyard, turn right along a gravelled track. Now ignore a path on the left, continuing past Dumworth Farm. Just after the farm the track bends right and soon you are heading towards the Downs: on reaching a T-junction, turn left along a lane. After 250 yards, turn right, downhill, along a track signed 'Warren Farm'. At a track junction, bear left along the main track. Do not take the path on the left: instead, continue ahead to reach a track junction. Turn right along the Ridgeway following it, as it descends gradually, for approximately a mile to reach the entrance to Warren Farm. Here the Ridgeway becomes metalled: continue ahead for another $^1/_2$ mile, then look for a house on the right called 'Wynders'. Just past the house, turn right along an enclosed footpath. Level at first, the path soon starts to ascend gradually between hedgerows, then through open fields. At Kiddington Cottage, bear to the left of the cottage, and continue along the path which ascends fairly steeply through Westridge Copse. The track levels out at the top and continues, through a farmyard, to reach the B4009.

The shorter walk turns right here, following the road through Westridge Green to reach a sharp left-hand bend. Here, go straight ahead, passing a postbox on the left. After passing the last house on the left the track becomes gravelled: after 200 yards, turn left along a path across the middle of a field. At the far side, go over at a cross-tracks, through a gap in a hedge, and bear left across the next field. At the far corner, continue along an enclosed path to reach a road. Turn right to return to the Bell Inn.

The longer walk turns left, then, after 100 yards, just past a chevron sign, turns right down a track. Where the track turns left to Gould's Cottage, go straight ahead along an ascending track between hedgerows. Where the track turns right into a field, carry straight on through a narrow strip of woodland. The path bears right, crosses a small opening and then ascends through College Wood. At the top, go through a barrier and bear right to reach a footpath junction. Here, turn right along a bridleway, with a field on your right, following it to reach a road. Turn right along the road for 700 yards to reach a road junction. Turn right along a road signed for Aldworth and, after 700 yards, turn left along a gravelled byway, following it through the trees. Go past houses, on the left, and continue along the track to reach the B4009. Turn left, then, after 100 yards, turn right at a road junction. Follow the road uphill, passing St Mary's Church, on the left, to return to the Bell Inn.

POINTS OF INTEREST:

Aldworth – The village has close connections with the poet, Alfred, Lord Tennyson, who, in 1850, married Emily Sellwood, who lived in nearby Pibworth Manor.

St Mary's Church - The church dates from the 12th century and is famous for the 14th-century monuments of the De la Beche family. The Aldworth Giants – as they are known - consist of nine recumbent stone figures. The figures represent three generations of the De la Beche family who lived during the 13th and 14th centuries.

REFRESHMENTS:
The Bell Inn, Aldworth.

Walk 64   **MAPLEDURHAM** $5^1/_4$m ($8^1/_2$km)

Maps: OS Sheets Landranger 175; Pathfinder 1172.

Views of rolling countryside en-route to the tiny hamlet of
Mapledurham. One small ascent.

Start: At 692781, the Packhorse Inn on the A4074.

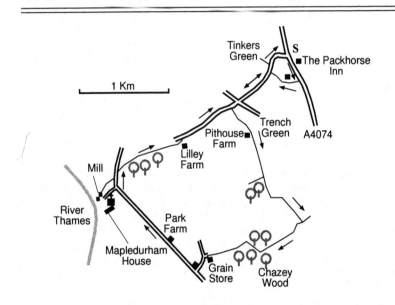

If you use the inn car park, please check with the landlord beforehand. From the inn,
turn left along the A4074, with care, to reach Greendean Farm, on the right. Just past
the farmhouse, turn right along a track, passing some old hen houses on the right, to
reach a minor road. There is a thatched cottage on the corner. Turn left and follow the
road to a crossroads. Go straight across and, after 50 yards, turn left along a concrete
track towards Trench Green. At the house on right, continue ahead until the track
bends left. Here, go through a gap in the hedge and maintain direction across a field,
ascending gently to reach a gap in the far corner. Go through and head towards the
left corner of a small wood. Here, ignore the main track which bends to the right, and
keep straight on along a path, descending gently, to the left of the wood, to reach a
stile.

Cross and head down the field beyond. Do not veer left: instead, keep straight ahead to drop down into a dip with a good view of the flat meadows near the River Thames to the right. Cross the dip and climb steeply to reach a stile. Go over and maintain direction across a field to reach a stile on to a lane. Turn right and follow the lane through Chazey Wood. An interesting variety of plant-life can be seen either side of the lane. The lane bends right, then left as it leaves the wood and descends, fairly steeply at first: continue down the road, passing a storage barn on the left, to reach a T-junction. Turn left and, at the next T-junction, turn right along a bridleway towards **Mapledurham House**. Follow the lane/bridleway to reach a road by a telephone box. To see the almshouses and visit **St Margaret's Church** turn left. Our route continues ahead along the road. After 50 yards, on the left, is the long entrance track to Mapledurham House and the **Mill**. After another 50 yards, turn right, up some steps to a high stile. Cross and go up the right edge of a field to reach a gap at the edge of a wood. Go through into the next field and walk ahead, with the wood on your right. Just before the wood ends, bear slightly left and go through a gate. Head up the next field, passing to the left of a small pond, to reach a farmyard gate. Go through and turn left to reach a road.

Turn right and follow the road to a crossroads. Go straight across and retrace your steps back to the thatched cottage you passed earlier on the walk. Continue on along the road to reach the A4074 and turn right to return to the Packhorse Inn, which will be on the left, crossing the road with great care.

POINTS OF INTEREST:

Mapledurham House – The house was built in about 1585 by Sir Richard Blount and is one of the largest Elizabethan houses in Oxfordshire. Fortified by Sir Charles Blount, for the King, during the Civil War it was taken by the Parliamentarians in 1643. It is open on Saturday, Sunday and Bank Holidays from Easter Sunday to the end of September, from 2.30-5pm.

St Margaret's Church, Mapledurham – The church dates from 1254-1289. The clock on the tower was a present from William IV in 1832. It has his initials, W R, on the clock face.

Mapledurham Watermill – Situated in the grounds of Mapledurham House, this is the last working corn and grist mill on the River Thames. The oldest parts date from the 15th century. Opening times are as for the House.

REFRESHMENTS:

The Packhorse Inn, Chazey Heath.
Mapledurham House Tearoom – Open during the season only.

Walk 65　　**STANFORD DINGLEY**　　5$\frac{1}{4}$m (8$\frac{1}{2}$km)

Maps: OS Sheets Landranger 174; Pathfinder 1171 and 1187.

A fairly easy walk in a picturesque part of the Pang River Valley.

Start: At 576715, the Bull Inn, Stanford Dingley.

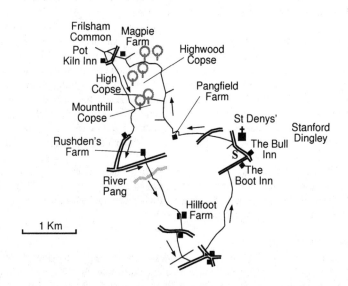

If you use the inn car park, please check with the landlord beforehand. From the inn turn right to **St Denys' Church**. Directly opposite the weather-boarded tower, turn left over a stile and go diagonally right across two fields. At the far side, cross a track and the stile opposite and go ahead, keeping a hedge on your left, to reach a road. Turn left for 70 yards, then go right over a stile and follow a path around two sides of the field beyond. When the fence line ends, continue ahead along an unfenced track towards Pangfield Farm. Just before the farm entrance, turn right for 40 yards, then turn left along the left edge of a field to reach the back of the farm buildings. Just beyond the field corner, turn right up a sunken track. Now, when the main track turns left, walk ahead through trees to reach a gate. Cross the meadow beyond to reach a small metal gate in a fence. Go half-left across the next field, heading towards a wood. Do not enter the wood: instead, turn left along its edge and, when it ends, cross a stile, turn right for 20 yards, then go left, through a gate, and cross a Christmas tree plantation. Leave the plantation and go ahead along a wide track, with larger Christmas trees on the right. The track bends right and soon ascends, passing to the left of Magpie Farm. Continue ahead along a drive to a lane. Cross the stile opposite and go up through three paddocks to reach a wood. Enter the wood and turn left along its inside edge. When you reach a wide track, turn left, downhill, to reach a road junction near the Pot Kiln Inn. Turn left for 110 yards, then turn right over a stile and follow the left edge of a field, down, and then up to a stile by a wood. Follow a rising path through the wood. Go straight over at two cross-tracks, eventually descending to join a lane near an old red-brick house on the right. Continue down the lane to reach a road and turn left. After 650 yards, opposite the entrance to Rushden's Farm, turn right along an enclosed path to the River Pang. Cross a bridge and turn left, following the field edge around to a gate in the far corner. Go through and follow the right edge of several fields to Hillfoot Farm. Go through the farmyard to reach a road. Turn right, downhill, and, after 110 yards, just after passing Hillfoot Cottage on the left, turn left up a fairly steep path. At the top, continue ahead along a drive to a T-junction. Bear left and walk to a road. Cross to the pavement opposite and turn left. Take the next road on the left and, after 100 yards, turn right along bridleway (Orchard View sign).

When the gravel ends continue ahead, passing apple trees and a line of poplars. Go through a gate and along the left edge of a large field. Just before the field corner, go through a gate and down a sunken path to a road. Turn right, go past the **Boot Inn** and, just before reaching a road junction, turn left along a narrow enclosed path. Now cross the River Pang, near an old mill, to reach a road opposite the **Bull Inn**.

POINTS OF INTEREST:

St Denys' Church – The current building dates from about 1200. Restoration work in 1870 revealed wall paintings and frescoes which were dated to the 13th century. The village of Stanford Dingley is named after William de Stanford (1224) and Richard Dyneley (1428).

The Boot Inn – This 16th century inn is reputedly haunted by a man who hanged himself in the orchard.

The Bull Inn – This 15th century coaching inn is noted for an antique game known as 'Ring the Bull'.

REFRESHMENTS:

The Bull Inn, Stanford Dingley.

The Pot Kiln, Frilsham Common.

The Blade Bone, Chapel Row.

Walk 66   HOOK NORTON $5\frac{1}{4}$m ($8\frac{1}{2}$km)

Maps: OS Sheets Landranger 151; Pathfinder 1044.

From the village of 'Old Nookey' (one of the local brewery's ales), this walk tours the area to the south-east of the village.

Start: At 355331, Hook Norton Parish Church.

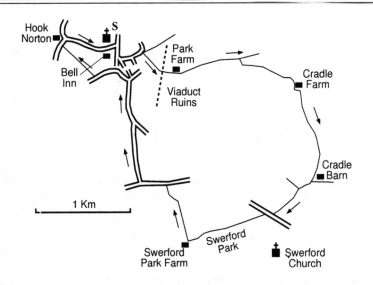

With your back to the church, turn left along the High Street and, after 50 yards, opposite the Village Shop, turn right down Bell Hill. At the bottom, take the left fork over a bridge and turn left along Park Road. At the road junction, with the Catholic Chapel on the right, continue straight ahead. When the road bends left, continue ahead along a bridleway, passing the remains of an old **railway viaduct**.

Just beyond Park Farm, on the left, and near a cattle grid, veer left to reach a gate. Go through and follow the track beyond to reach a second gate. Go through and continue ahead, soon ignoring a waymarked track on the left and bearing right, with the main track, downhill, to cross a small stream. When the track ends, continue along the left edge of a field, heading towards Cradle Farm. Go through a gate to the right of the house, and, keeping the house on your left, continue to reach a gate and drive, on the left.

Turn right along the drive. Now, where the metalled drive bends left, near the farm buildings, turn right along a farm track which soon bends left, uphill. At the top, to your left you can see the village of Swerford. Continue along the track to reach a road. Cross, with care, go through the gate opposite, and continue along a bridleway. You now have a closer view of Swerford, on your left.

At the far end of the bridleway, go through a gate and bear left for 10 yards to reach the drive of Swerford Park. Turn right for 50 yards, passing a house on the left and then turning right, through gates, to go along a second drive. Follow this to reach a road. Turn left to reach a road junction. Turn right. Soon the village of **Hook Norton** comes into view. At the next road junction, turn left downhill.

As you enter the village, bear left, uphill, towards a row of stone cottages. Follow the road round as it bends left, then, just before a speed de-regulation sign, turn right over a stile. Bear left down a field to reach, and cross, two stiles in the bottom left-hand corner. Continue along the right-hand edge of a couple of fields, with a small stream on the right, to reach a road. Turn right to reach a green. The Pear Tree Inn is on your left here. To see **Hook Norton Brewery**, go straight across and up the road opposite. Now take the first turning on the left, Brewery Lane. The Brewery buildings soon come into view. Retrace your steps to the Pear Tree Inn road junction and turn left along the pavement to return to the Parish Church of St Peter, on the left. The Bell Inn is just opposite.

POINTS OF INTEREST:
Railway Viaduct – The Cheltenham-Banbury railway line once crossed the valley along this 80 foot viaduct.

Hook Norton – Over 50 years ago the village had an ironworks and some ironstone quarries, but it is now better known for its brewery, where the well-known 'Old Nookey' beer is brewed.

Hook Norton Brewery – The business started in 1849 as a maltings for local barley. It was only in 1872 that brewing began. It has continued ever since. The Brewery is not open to the public, but there is a shop.

REFRESHMENTS:
The Bell Inn, Hook Norton.
The Pear Tree Inn, Hook Norton.

Walk 67   **CROPREDY**   5¹/₄m (8¹/₂km)

Maps: OS Sheets Landranger 151; Pathfinder 1022.
Canal tow-path, rural footpaths and a historical site combine to make a pleasant walk.
Start: At 468465, the Brasenose Arms, Cropredy.

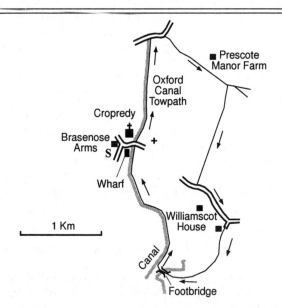

If you use the inn car park, please check with the landlord beforehand. With your back to the inn, go left of the green (The Plantation), then bear left along the road passing the Old Coal Wharf, on the right, to reach a bridge over the canal. Cross the bridge and turn right to reach the canal tow-path. Turn right under the road bridge and follow the tow-path, soon passing **Cropredy Church**, on the other side of the canal. Go under a second bridge and continue past a lock. You are likely to see a number of attractive boats along the canal here. Continue along the tow-path to reach bridge No. 150 and lock No. 24. Here, bear right away from the tow-path to reach a road. Turn right along the road and, at a sharp left-hand bend, go straight ahead through two gates, and across the middle of two fields.

At the far side of the second field, with Prescote Manor Farm on your left, cross a farm track and continue along a track on the other side. The track crosses a stream, then runs through a narrow belt of trees before continuing along the left edge of a field. At the far side, go through a gap and immediately bear right across the middle of the next field. At the far side, turn right along a fairly wide track, walking with a hedge and ditch on the left, to cross three fields. At the far corner of the third field, go straight ahead, through a gate, and along the right edge of the field beyond to reach a road. There is a barn in the field on the right. Turn left and follow the road through Williamscot, passing the entrance to Williamscot House and some attractive stone cottages on the right.

Just as you leave the village, turn right along a 'No Through Road'. Where the road bends left, go straight ahead past a barrier and gates. There is a farm on the right. Go through the next gate and along the left edge of a field, which, level at first, drops down at the far side. Here, go through a gate and across the middle of the next field. The track now bears left towards the A361. Follow it around for about 20 yards, then turn right and walk across the middle of the field, heading diagonally away from the road. At the far side, go through a gate and bear right across the next field to reach, and cross, a bridge over the River Cherwell.

Continue ahead up the next field to reach a canal bridge. Cross a stile, to the left of the bridge, then go down some steps to reach the tow-path. Turn right and follow the tow-path back to the Cropredy Road Bridge (No. 153). Here, bear right up to the road (the Bridge Stores is just opposite) and turn left to cross the bridge, retracing your steps back to the Brasenose Arms.

POINTS OF INTEREST:
Cropredy Church – In 1644 Parliamentarian troops under General Waller intercepted a party of Royalists near the river. Some of the soldiers who were killed are buried in the churchyard. If you visit the church, look closely at the lectern. It was thrown into the river and was not recovered until 30 years later. One foot of the lectern was found to be missing and was replaced. However, when the lectern was cleaned it was found to be made of brass whereas the replacement foot had been made of bronze. To this day the lectern has one bronze and two brass feet.

REFRESHMENTS:
The Brasenose Arms, Cropredy.
The Old Coal Wharf serves teas, but please check the opening times.

Walk 68   **UPPER LAMBOURN** $5\frac{1}{4}$m ($8\frac{1}{2}$km)

Maps: OS Sheets Landranger 174; Pathfinder 1170/1154.

A walk on the Berkshire Downs, deep in the heart of racehorse training country.

Start: At 318799, the Malt Shovel Inn, Upper Lambourn.

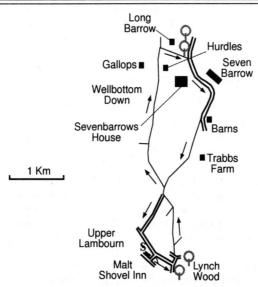

If you use the inn car park, please check with the landlord beforehand. From the inn car park, turn left to reach a road junction. Turn right along a lane, with a ditch on the right, to reach a T-junction. Turn left, uphill, along the Lambourn Valley Way, following it through part of Lynch Wood. Ignore a track on the right, continuing along the road to reach the entrance to stables, on the left. Swing right with the road and continue uphill. The road ascends fairly steeply and, as it levels out, becomes more of a track. Soon you will have glimpses of the surrounding countryside as the hedgerow diminishes.

At a track junction, bear left to reach another junction. Here, turn right along a byway. After 100 yards, fork left along a track between hedgerows. To your left are some horse gallops and, beyond these, in the distance, you can see the countryside of Wiltshire. Soon views open out to the right too.

When a wider track joins from the left, continue ahead for 20 yards, then fork right along a narrower track to reach a barn on the left. Keeping the barn on your left, continue straight ahead along the byway. Soon you will be able to see a radio transmitter on a hill ahead and to the right. The track eventually emerges into open countryside. There are fine, panoramic, views from here. When another track joins from the left, continue ahead, downhill. There are gallops on the left and a field with jump fences on the right. At the far end of the field with the jumps, turn right along a track. The track goes over a mound just to the right of some trees: this mound is part of a large long barrow. Continue along the track to reach a road.

Turn right along the road. You are now in the area of the **Seven Barrows**. See how many you can spot in the fields to your left as you follow the road around a long right-hand bend. Continue past Postdown Farm barns, on the left, then, when the road bends left, bear slightly right up a track, gradually ascending to the Downs again. As the track levels out it becomes narrower: at the top, where a track joins from the right, continue ahead to reach a junction. Go straight on, down a tree-lined track and, on reaching a T-junction at the bottom, turn left along Fulke Walwyn Way. At the far end, continue along the road through the village. At the next junction, turn right to return to the Malt Shovel Inn.

POINTS OF INTEREST:
Lambourn Seven Barrows – Despite the name, there are actually about 30 or 40 Bronze Age barrows in this area. One of the best groups is seen in the fields on the left of this walk. This group contains six bowl barrows, two saucer barrows and one disc barrow. The disc barrows were primarily for women, while the bowl barrows were for people of either sex. The barrows were constructed of chalk which made them stand out against the landscape. The area is now a Nature Reserve and a designated Site of Special Scientific Interest.

REFRESHMENTS:
The Malt Shovel Inn, Upper Lambourn. The building is thought to date from the early 17th century.

Maps: OS Sheets Landranger 151; Pathfinder 1045.
From the hilltop village of Deddington, this walk goes across
farmland and along old tracks.
Start: At 466316, Deddington Market Place.

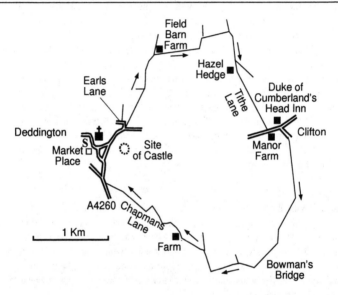

From the Market Place, **Deddington**, take the road which passes to the right of the
Church of St Peter and St Paul. The road turns right to reach a T-junction. Turn left
along the B4031. The site of **Deddington Castle** is over to the right. At the junction
with Earls Lane, cross the road and go over a stile. Go along a path which bears left
across the middle of a field, keeping to the left of a clump of trees to reach a footbridge
at the far side. Cross and bear right across the next field. Go through a gate and turn
left along a concrete track. At Field Barn Farm, keep to the right of the farmhouse,
passing between two barns and going along a farm track. At a T-junction, turn left
and follow a track. Go past a footpath on the left and continue downhill to a T-junction.
Turn right along a track (Tithe Lane), following it to reach a road (the B4031) at
Clifton. Turn left past a disused church, now a consultancy business.

At the Duke of Cumberland's Head Inn, on the left, turn right down Chapel Close. Where the road bends right, bear left of 'Manor Barn' , and go down an enclosed bridleway signed 'Somerton $2^1/_4$'. Follow the bridleway which soon becomes a green lane. As you follow it, look to your left to catch glimpses of a viaduct carrying the Banbury/Marylebone railway. Beyond a right-hand bend, go over at a cross-tracks and continue along a field edge. At the far end, go through a gap in the hedge and turn left along the field edge, walking with a ditch on your left. At the field corner, turn right and follow the left edge of two fields and go through a gate near a stream. Bowman's Bridge is a few yards to the left. Do not go over the bridge: instead, turn right up the edge of the field, heading away from the stream. After 150 yards, veer left across the field to reach a gate at the far side. Go through and cross the middle of the next field.

Go through a gap and along the edge of the next field and, just before the far corner, turn right along a wide, enclosed track. Where the hedge on the left ends, turn left along a track towards some farm buildings, passing to the left of a pond. Keep to the right of the farm to join a metalled farm track. Go past some barns, on the left, and, at a junction, bear left. After 100 yards, turn right along a farm track, staying on the main track as it gradually ascends to reach a road (the A4260). Turn right and, after 50 yards, turn right again up St Thomas Street. At the next road junction, go straight on, uphill, to reach a T-junction. Turn left to return to the Market Place.

POINTS OF INTEREST:
Deddington – The village was once an important trading centre for cattle, sheep and horses. Old records show that during the 18th and 19th century as many as 600 or 700 horses changed hands during the 'Pudding and Pie' fair held in November.
Church of St Peter and St Paul, Deddington – Parts of the church date back to the 13th century. The tower had to be rebuilt following its collapse in 1635. The church's prominent position, on the hilltop, makes its tower visible for miles around.
Deddington Castle – Only the grassy ramparts now remain of the 12th-century castle, so if you decide to visit you will need a good imagination. The site is maintained by English Heritage.

REFRESHMENTS:
The Duke of Cumberland's Head Inn, Clifton.
There are numerous possibilities in Deddington.

Walk 70　　**FARINGDON FOLLY**　　$5\frac{1}{4}$m ($8\frac{1}{2}$km)

Maps: OS Sheets Landranger 164; Pathfinder 1135.

An undulating walk, including the ascent of Faringdon Hill, the site of an Iron Age fort, a Cromwellian battery, and the last major folly to be built in England.

Start: At 312971, Littleworth Church car park.

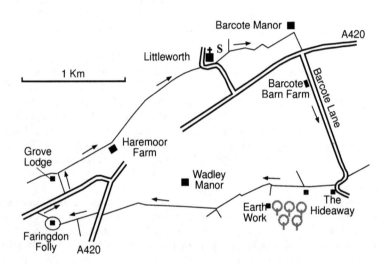

From the car park, with the church on your left, take the bridleway to the right of a house, signed 'Buckland 2'. After 30 yards, fork right, passing a sign stating 'Pedestrians Only', to reach a playing field. Go along the right edge of the field, and continue along an enclosed path. At a path junction, go through a squeeze stile and head down a field, passing about 30 yards to the left of a waterworks enclosure. At the bottom of the field, cross a stile and footbridge, then go up the next field, keeping to the left of a hedge. At the top right-hand corner, turn right, through a gate, and go along the left edge of the field beyond. After 50 yards, turn left over two stiles, then cross the middle of a field to reach the drive of Barcote Manor. Turn right to reach the A420. Cross, with care, and continue along the road opposite, passing Barcote Barn

Farm on the right. There are some good views ahead. Now ignore a bridleway on the left, following the minor road as it bends right towards a house called 'The Hideaway'.

When the road bends left, with the house on the left, continue straight ahead along a farm track, passing some barns on the left. After a further 400 yards there are some earthworks on the left, though these, the site of an Iron Age fort, are not easy to identify. At a track junction, bear slightly left over an earth bridge, and continue along the field edge, keeping the hedge to your right. At the far corner, go over a metal bar stile, just to the right of a gate, and bear diagonally right across two fields to reach the right edge of a small wood. Here, cross another bar stile, and then bear left along the left edge of a field. In the trees, on the hilltop ahead, you may be able to see Faringdon Folly. On reaching the A420, cross, with care, and go over the stile opposite, signed 'Faringdon 1'. Bear left up a field to reach the left edge of a small copse. Continue up the right edge of the next field. On looking left you may be able to see, in the distance, the White Horse of Uffington. At the top of the field, go over a crossing track and continue into the trees for 40 yards to reach **Faringdon Folly**.

Retrace your steps to the crossing track and turn left. There are panoramic views of the area as you walk around the folly boundary. When you reach a hedge, on the right, turn right down the field edge. At the hedge corner, continue on down to reach a road. Cross, with care, and turn right. After 300 yards, turn left over a stile, signed 'Smokedown 2', and go down a farm track. Just past a house on the left, at a footpath junction, turn right over a stile. Now go along the left edge of a field, continuing ahead to pass to the left of Haremoor Farm. Go over two stiles and bear left, under some telegraph wires, to reach a stile in the right-hand fence. Cross and turn left for 40 yards, then bear diagonally right across two fields. At the far side of the second field, go over a stile and turn right along a track. After 25 yards, turn left to reach a road. Continue along the road and in 250 yards turn left back into the church car park.

POINTS OF INTEREST:
Faringdon Folly – The folly is thought to be the last major folly tower to have been built in Britain. It is 100 feet high and was built in 1935 by the 14th Lord Berners, an eccentric musician and author. Faringdon Hill, on which the folly is built, has quite a distinguished history: it is also the site of a Cromwellian battery, placed here during the siege on Faringdon, and the site of an Iron Age fort.

REFRESHMENTS:
The Fox and Hounds, Littleworth.

Walk 71   SONNING   5¼m (8½km)

Maps:·OS Sheets Landranger 175; Pathfinder 1172.

A walk which takes in a path through a Bluebell Copse, a visit to a church where the poet Tennyson was married and a stroll beside the River Thames.

Start: At 746767, the Flowing Spring Inn, Sonning.

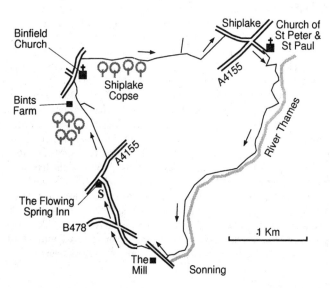

If you use the inn car park, please check with the landlord beforehand. From the car park, turn left to reach the A4155. Turn right. This is the main Reading to Henley road and can be busy, so keep to the verge and take care. A new path is being created on the opposite side of the road but, at the time of writing, it is not open. After 220 yards, cross the road, with even greater care, and bear left between two new wooden fences. At the end, bear right up an enclosed bridleway signed 'Binfield Heath 1'. The path ascends gradually between hedgerows. Cross a farm track and go through a small wooded area. Continue with a copse on your left and a field on your right. At the top, continue between fences to reach a footpath junction. Go straight on, following a track to reach a road. Radbrook House is on your right. Turn right along the road, passing Binfield Heath Congregational Church on the right. Continue for another 200 yards, then turn right along a footpath signed 'Shiplake $1^1/_2$'.

The path passes around an old kissing gate, then continues along the right edge of a field and, at the far corner, enters Shiplake Copse. Follow the path down through the wood, which has lots of bluebells during Spring. On emerging from the wood, bear left along the left edge of a field. At the corner, continue ahead across the field, ascending gradually, then go along the left edge of the field, now walking with a hedge on your left, to reach a cross-tracks. Go straight ahead and, on reaching a power-line post, bear left and follow a line of power posts. Ignore a path on the left and continue ahead, with the power lines just to your left, to reach a footpath sign. Turn right along the field edge, walking with a wire fence on your left. At the next footpath sign, go over a stile on the left and walk across the field beyond, heading towards Shiplake. At the far side of the field, go through a narrow gap between electric fences, to reach a gate. Go through and follow the track beyond to reach a road.

Turn right and follow the road to the A4155. The Plowden Arms Inn is on the right. Bear left across the road, with care, and go down Church Lane opposite to reach the **Church of St Peter and St Paul**, on the left. Go past the church and bear right down a stepped path. At the bottom, turn left along a track and follow it to reach the River Thames. Here, turn right and, with the river on your left, follow the Thames Path to reach the road at Sonning. Turn right, passing the entrance to the **Mill Theatre** on the left. Cross the road and continue ahead to reach the French Horn car park. Here, bear left along an enclosed footpath to reach a road. Turn left, then right, through Sonning Eye to reach a road junction. Continue ahead, following the road to its end. Go through a gate, cross and continue along the road opposite. After 150 yards, go over a stile on the right and bear left along the edge of two fields. The path runs parallel with the road, just the other side of the hedge. At the far end of the field, cross a stile on the left and turn right along the road to return to the Flowing Spring Inn, on the left.

POINTS OF INTEREST:
The Church of St Peter and St Paul, Shiplake – Alfred Lord Tennyson was married at this church on 13th June, 1850.
Mill Theatre – The mill was in use from Saxon times, closing for the first time in 1969. It is now a Theatre and Restaurant and well worth a visit.

REFRESHMENTS:
The Flowing Spring Inn, Sonning.
The Plowden Arms Inn, Shiplake.

Walk 72   WESTON-ON-THE-GREEN $5^{1}/_{4}$m ($8^{1}/_{2}$km)

Maps: OS Sheets Landranger 164; Pathfinder 1092.

Across fields, through Bletchingdon and Kirtlington Parks,
returning along the Oxfordshire Way.

Start: At 531186, the Village Hall car park, Weston-on-the Green.

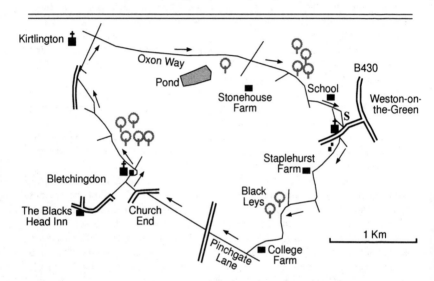

From the car park, turn left to reach a road junction. Turn right along Church Lane,
with the **church** on your right. After 150 yards, turn left, and go through a kissing
gate. After a further 20 yards, turn right along an enclosed path. Go over a stile and
bear left across the middle of the field beyond. At the far side, cross a small stream
and head for Staplehurst Farm. At the field corner, turn left along the field edge and,
at the far corner, cross a stile on the right. Do not go over the stile on the left: instead,
go along the left edge of two fields to reach a corner of Black Leys Wood. Cross a
stile on the left and head along the right edge of the next two fields. About 50 yards
before the far corner of the second field, turn right over a small wooden bridge. Cross
the middle of the field beyond and go through a gap in the hedge, to the right of
College Farm. Bear left, then right, along the field edge to reach a stile in the far
corner. Cross and turn right to reach a track junction. Here, turn right, along Pinchgate
Lane, to reach a road.

140

Bear left, across the road, and go along the path opposite (signed 'Bletchingdon $^1/_2$'), following the left edge of a large field. Cross a small bridge at the far side, and head across the next field to reach a tree-lined hedge corner. Go through a gate in the hedge, and head up the left edge of a small plantation to reach a road. Turn left, and, at a sharp left-hand bend, continue straight ahead along a lane (signed 'To the Church') to reach St Giles' Church. (To visit Bletchingdon, and its inn, turn left and follow a path, and then a road to reach a large village green.) Turn right, past the church, and enter Bletchingdon Park. Just past a large garage, on the left, go over a stile to the left of a private road and immediately turn left along the field edge. Cross a stile in far fence and head across the next field to its far right-hand corner. Cross a stile and veer right across the field beyond. Go through a gap and turn left along a field edge. At the far side, go through a wide gap and turn right, walking with a hedge on your right. After 150 yards, bear diagonally left across two fields to reach a road. Turn right and, after 50 yards, just before a house on the right, turn right through a gate. Bear left, cross a drive and go through the gate opposite. Now follow a well-defined path across Kirtlington Park. After 400 yards, veer right on to the Oxfordshire Way. The path is not very clear, but crosses the field, diagonally, to reach a stile and footbridge. Cross these, and bear right across the next field. At the far side go through a gap in the hedge.

Go past a small copse, on your left, and, when it ends continue across two fields. Go through Long Plantation and across a wild meadow. At a cross-tracks, turn right, and, after 20 yards, turn left, and cross a field to reach the edge of a wood. Bear right along the wood's edge, then, about 50 yards before the far corner of the field on the right, turn left over a footbridge. Cross another wild meadow, go over a stream, and, after 5 yards, turn right over a stile. Bear left across a field and, at a corner, go ahead for 30 yards, then turn right across the field to reach a stile between new and old bungalows. Go along the enclosed path beyond to reach a lane. Turn left and follow the lane back to the village hall.

POINTS OF INTEREST:
Weston-on-the-Green Church – Possibly 11th-century, the church contains a 12th-century font, a masthead cross from a Spanish Armada ship, and an 18th-century canvas by Battoni (1708-1787). Weston village is reputedly haunted by three ghosts.

REFRESHMENTS:
The Blacks Head Inn, Bletchingdon.
The Ben Jonson Inn, Weston-on-the-Green.

Walks 73 & 74   SHIPTON-UNDER-WYCHWOOD $5\frac{1}{4}$m ($8\frac{1}{2}$km)
or $7\frac{1}{4}$m ($11\frac{1}{2}$km)

Maps: OS Sheets Landranger 163; Pathfinder 1091 and 1068.
An undulating walk providing some fine views.
Start: At 279179, the Church of St Mary the Virgin, Shipton.

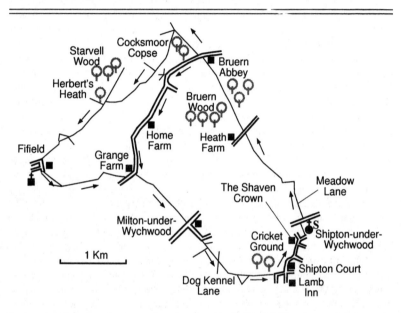

Facing the **church**, take the enclosed path to the left and follow it to reach the main road. Cross, with care, and turn right. After 75 yards, turn left along Meadow Lane (signed for the Oxfordshire Way), and, at the far end, cross a stream and continue along a track. Just before the track enters a field, turn left through a gap (there is a blue arrow waymarker) and go along the left edge of a field. After 150 yards, turn right along a clearly defined path across the field. Cross a stile and continue across two more fields, then go along an enclosed path to reach a road. Heath Farm is over to your left here. Cross the road and go through the gate opposite to continue along an enclosed path. Go through a gate and along the left edge of a field. At the far corner, go through a gap in the hedge, then through a gate, and then bear right along a wide ride through Bruern Wood, heading towards Bruern Abbey. Go through a gate and bear left across a field to reach a stile. Cross and continue ahead to reach the left corner of the Abbey grounds. Here, bear left across the field to reach a road.

The shorter walk turns left along the road. After 600 yards, just beyond a left-hand bend, bear right at a road junction, following a road signed 'Fifield $2^1/_2$'. Follow the road for almost a mile to reach Grange Farm on the right. Here, turn left, through a gate, on to a bridleway, rejoining the longer route.

The longer walk crosses the road and goes through the gate opposite. Go along the left edge of a field and, at the far corner, go through a gate and continue through a wood. Just before a field on the left, turn left along a narrow path, following it to reach a minor road. Turn left, then, after 10 yards, turn right, over a footbridge. Go along the edge of the field beyond to reach a crossing farm track. Turn right, then immediately left along a field edge. The track bends right, then left. At the next cross-tracks, turn right through a gap, and go left along a field edge. Keep ahead through a wood to reach a track junction. Here, turn left, but, after 30 yards, where the main track turns right, go straight on, following Darcy Dalton Way to reach a road at Fifield. Turn left to reach a road junction. Go straight ahead, passing Fifield House on the left. Go through a gate and cross three fields. At the far side, go through a gate and turn left across the next field. At the far side, turn left along the field edge. Go through a gate, and bear right across the field beyond to reach a gate just to the right of some cottages. Turn left along a lane and, after 150 yards, at Grange Farm, turn right through a gate, rejoining the shorter route.

Follow the signed bridleway and, when the track ends, continue across fields to reach houses and a road at Milton-under-Wychwood. Turn right, then, after 30 yards, turn left along Jubilee Lane, following it to its end. Go through a gate and cross two fields. Go over a stile and footbridge in the far corner of second field, then bear right up a fence-enclosed path. At the top of a rise, bear left along an enclosed farm track, which becomes gravelled (Dog Kennel Lane), to reach a road. Continue ahead, then go around a sharp left-hand bend, passing **Shipton Court** on your right. After 700 yards, bear right to return to the church.

POINTS OF INTEREST:

The Church of St Mary the Virgin – The 12th-century church stands on the site of what is thought to have been a Minster in Saxon times.

Shipton Court – The Court was built in 1603 by Sir Rowland de Lacy. It is one of the largest Jacobean houses in the country.

REFRESHMENTS:

The Shaven Crown, Shipton-under-Wychwood.

Walk 75   **COOKHAM AND WINTER HILL** $5^1/_2$m ($8^3/_4$km)
Maps: OS Sheets Landranger 175; Explorer 3.
This varied walk, near the birthplace of the artist Sir Stanley
Spencer, takes you across ancient meadows, along the River
Thames and up Winter Hill for some fine views.
Start: At 894853, Cookham Moor car park.

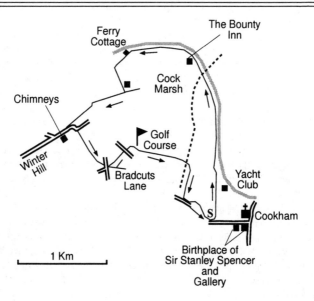

Facing the village, walk half-left, as signed 'Footpath to **Cockmarsh**' to reach a swing
gate. Go through and cross the field beyond, heading towards a solitary tree on the
river-bank. Keep left of the Yacht Club and, at the river's edge, turn left along the
tow-path. Pass under a railway bridge, noting the National Trust information sign on
the left, and go through a swing gate. Continue past some cottages, and the Bounty
Inn, staying on the tow-path until you reach Ferry Cottage. Here, bear left, away from
the river and, after 200 yards, turn left across a field. At the far side, pass a pond on
the left and go over a stone stile. After 50 yards, at the foot of the hill, turn right along
a well-defined track leading, fairly steeply, up towards **Winter Hill**. As you ascend
there are some good views of the Thames and the Chilterns beyond. On reaching a

road, opposite a house called 'Chimneys', turn left to follow the road to a sharp left-hand bend. Here, go ahead over a stile, just to the left of iron gate with a sign 'Winter Hill Farm'. Cross a stone stile and go along an enclosed path, following a line of telegraph posts. Cross two more stiles and continue ahead to reach a road. Bear left, crossing Bradcutts Lane to reach a signposted stile.

Go along the enclosed path beyond to reach another stile. Cross and bear left along the left edge of the field beyond to reach a stile in the corner. Cross the stile and the road beyond, with care, to reach a path opposite, just to the left of the entrance gates to September Grange. Follow the path to reach a junction of paths with the Grange on the right. Here, ignore the footpath sign on the left and turn right, over a stile, and follow the track beyond down the right edge of a golf course. When the fence on the right ends, continue ahead across the golf course, passing to the left of a barn, to reach a railway bridge. Cross and then bear right along a track to reach a corner of the golf course. Cross a stile and walk ahead along a lane for 50 yards. Just before reaching a road, turn left along a narrow footpath between houses. At the bottom, cross a stile, and bear right along a wide track to reach a stile and footbridge. Cross these and then turn right to return to the car park.

A worthwhile extension to the walk visits **Cookham**: go along the road into the village. Sir Stanley Spencer's cottage is on the right, and there is a gallery, on the right, at the road junction. To visit the church, turn left at the junction, then left again.

POINTS OF INTEREST:

Cock Marsh – Cock Marsh is 132 acres of flat, marshy ground. Traces of human habitation going back over 4,000 years have been found in the area. The commons around Cookham are said to be haunted by Herne the Hunter.

Winter Hill – Owned by the National Trust, the summit provides a superb panorama of the River Thames between Marlow and Bourne End.

Cookham – Thought, now, to date back to Anglo-Saxon times, the village lives on the memory of Sir Stanley Spencer, the artist, who was born here. When walking down the High Street note the names of the cottages and also the plaque on Vine Cottage. The nave of Cookham Church dates from around 1140.

REFRESHMENTS:

The Bounty Inn, beside the River Thames, passed on the walk.
The Crown, Cookham, on the far side of the green near the car park.
There are many other opportunities along Cookham's High Street.

STOKE TALMAGE $5\frac{1}{2}$m ($9\frac{1}{2}$km)

Maps: OS Sheets Landranger 164; Pathfinder 1117 and 1137.

Following rarely used footpaths, this walk provides good views of the Chiltern Escarpment and the Oxfordshire Plain and passes close to the site of a lost village.

Start: At 678993, St Mary Magdelen Church, Stoke Talmage.

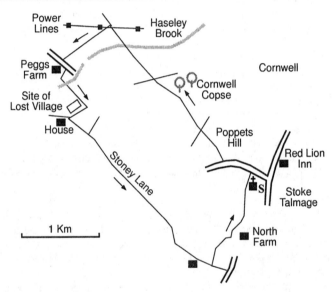

With your back to the church, turn left down the road, ignoring footpaths to both left and right. When the tarmac surface ends, continue along the lane. Cross a cattle grid and turn right over a wooden rail beside a gate. Follow the path beyond, with a hedge on the right, over Poppets Hill and down to a stile. Cross the stile, a farm road, and the stile opposite, and bear half-right across a large field to reach the left corner of Cornwell Copse. Go through a gate and walk with the copse on your right. When the edge of the copse bends right, bear left across the field towards the opposite corner. Go over a farm track and through a gate into a field. The path across this field is indistinct, so head for the far left-hand corner. Cross a stile and a footbridge over Haseley Brook and bear left across the next field to reach a gate. Go through and cross the field beyond, passing under power lines, to reach the left corner of a copse. Now, do not go ahead through the gap in the fence: instead, turn sharp left and go diagonally across the field, passing just to the right of a pylon. A little to the right of the opposite field corner, go through a gate and walk ahead along an enclosed farm track.

When the track bends left, go straight on, through an iron gate, and along the left edge of a field. Go through a second gate and head towards the buildings of Peggs Farm. Just before the buildings, go through a gate and turn left down a lane, keeping the buildings on your right. Just after the last building, turn right through a gate and bear half-left across a field to reach a stile and footbridge. Cross and go straight up the next field, aiming about 40 yards to the left of the conifer plantation on your right, to reach a stile in the top hedge. Cross and immediately turn right to follow the hedge on the right, at first, and then the edge of a plantation. The plantation is the site of the **lost village of Standhill**. At the end of the plantation, continue straight on across the field to reach **Stoney Lane** near a house.

Turn left along the track and follow it for the next 2 miles. The track becomes a green lane, then a tarmac road. On reaching two houses on the right, continue up the road for 250 yards, then turn left, up some steps, and go over a stile into a field. Follow the fence on the right to the far corner, cross a stile and go along the left edge of the small field beyond. Go to the left of a barn to reach a farm track. Turn left to reach a large barn, then turn right with the track and continue straight on along a narrow path passing between two rows of cottages. Cross a lawn to reach a stile. Bear diagonally left across the field beyond, keeping well to the left of North Farm. Cross a stile and a footbridge in the bottom corner and bear half-left across the next field to reach another stile and footbridge. Cross and follow the right field edge to the far corner. There, turn left to reach a stile on the right. Cross and follow the left-hand hedge through two paddocks to reach a road. Turn right back to the church.

POINTS OF INTEREST:
Lost Village of Standhill – Standhill is thought to have been a thriving village during the Middles Ages. The site, mainly hidden by the plantation, stretched between the plantation and the cottage at Stoney Lane. It was depopulated, probably by plague, during the 14th century.
Stoney Lane – This ancient road is thought to be over 1,000 years old.

REFRESHMENTS:
The Red Lion, Stoke Talmage.

Walk 77   **STANTON ST JOHN** $5^1/_2$m ($8^3/_4$km)

Maps: OS Sheets Landranger 164; Pathfinder 1116.

A fairly level walk through farmland and woods just north-east of Oxford, starting from a village where one of the Pilgrim Fathers was born.

Start: At 578093, Stanton St John Village Hall.

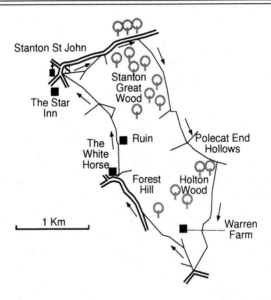

Please check locally before parking at the Village Hall. Go over the stile at the back of the car park and, bearing slightly left, take a path downhill to a footbridge, just left of two electricity poles. Cross and bear half-left to cross a stile and footbridge just to the right of the field corner. Now follow a line of power poles for 300 yards to reach a gate on the left. Go through on to Menmarsh Road. Turn right along the road for 600 yards, then turn right, through iron gate signed 'Holton $2^1/_2$'. Bear slightly left across a field to reach a corner of Stanton Great Wood, then continue ahead, keeping the wood on your right. Cross an earth bridge into the next field and continue along the wood edge to reach the very far corner. Go over another earth bridge and turn left, with a ditch on your left. following the edge of the ditch as it bends right. At the field corner, turn right (by a willow tree), and, after 20 yards, turn left over a ditch. Continue, still with a ditch on your left, to reach the far field corner. Go through a gap and continue to a stile on to Polecat Lane, part of an ancient road. Cross the lane and the stile opposite and follow the hedge on the right to reach a corner of Holton Wood. Bear left along a track for 200 yards, passing some farm buildings (Polecat End Hollows), then look for a red gate on the right. Turn right through the gate and follow a fire break up through Holton Wood.

At the far side, go straight on across the middle of two fields to reach a stile. Go over and bear slightly right to cross some stepping stones and a stile. Go straight on to the field corner, then follow the field's right edge to the far side. Bear slightly right across the next field to reach a hedge corner. Turn right through a gap and bear right across the next field to its far corner to reach a road. Turn right and almost immediately right again along the track to Warren Farm. Cross a cattle grid and, near a 'Private Road' sign, turn left across a field. At the far side, turn right and walk with a hedge on your left. Cross a stile and bear slightly right to cross another at the edge of a copse. Follow a zig-zag path through the copse and, on emerging, keep ahead along the right edge of a field. At the far side, cross a stile and a track and go through the gate opposite. Cross field beyond, with a copse on your right. When the copse ends, go straight ahead to reach a gate in the left-hand edge. Go through and turn right to follow a road, with care, through Forest Hill. Just before reaching the White Horse Inn, bear right along a track to reach Minchin Court. Here, turn right down a track for 80 yards, then turn left up some steps and go over a stile. Cross the field beyond, go over a stile and continue ahead, with a wire fence on your left. At the far field corner, turn right for 80 yards, then turn left over a wooden bridge. Bear left of a derelict farm building and go along the left edge of three fields. At the end of the third field, with some houses on your left, go over a stile and bear right across two fields to return to the car park. The **village church** is just beyond the car park.

POINTS OF INTEREST:
The Church of St John the Baptist, Stanton St John – The church was built in the 13th century. Inside there are carved bench ends of human heads or grotesque animals. Rectory Farm House, just across the road from the church, has a plaque over the door stating 'The birthplace of John White, 1575-1648, Fellow of New College, Oxford, and chief founder of the colony of Massachusetts, New England'.

REFRESHMENTS:
The White Horse Inn, Forest Hill.
The Star Inn, Stanton St John.

Walk 78 HERMITAGE 5¹/₂m (8³/₄km)

Maps: OS Sheets Landranger 174; Pathfinder 1171.

A mixture of farmland and woods, this undulating walk has plenty of interest.

Start: At 506729, Hermitage Village Hall.

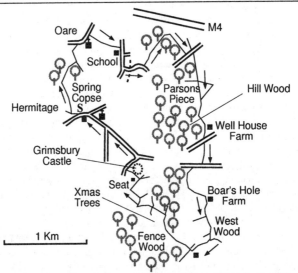

With your back to the village hall, turn right along the road and, after 50 yards, turn right up Doctor's Lane. Near the end of the high wall on the left, bear right over a stile. Go diagonally right across two fields to reach a stile at the edge of Spring Copse. Cross and follow a path through the copse, ascending gradually. At a footpath junction near the top, turn left. Go past a house on the left, continuing for a further 50 yards, then veering right along a narrow path through ferns into a small wood.

The path descends through trees to reach a lane at Oare. Here, turn right and continue to **St Bartholomew's Church**, on the right. After a further 50 yards, at Oare Cottage, turn right along a track. Go over a stile and along the left edge of a field. At the far corner, go over a stile and bear right across a field to reach a stile in the right-hand corner. Cross and turn right along a road. After 300 yards, turn left along Chapel Lane. After 50 yards, near a speed restriction sign, turn left down a narrow enclosed footpath. Cross over an old railway line (noting the bridge on your right), and continue through a play area to reach a lane. Continue straight on along the lane, but where it turns right, bear left along a footpath, passing Ivy Cottage on the left. Go over a stile and along the left edge of a field to reach another stile. Cross and follow the path beyond through a narrow band of trees, passing a pond on the left. At the far end you will see and hear cars whizzing along the M4, which is just over to your left.

Go over a stile and bear right across the corner of a field to reach a stile in the right-hand fence. Cross and go along the right edge of a field, with a wood (Chalkpit Piece) on your right, to reach a road. Turn left for 50 yards, then turn right along a broad track. Go straight over at a cross-tracks, ascending gradually to reach a track junction. Carry straight on along the main track, going through Hill Wood to reach a road. Cross and continue along the track opposite.

Just past two cottages on the right, turn right on a path across a meadow to reach a stile just to the right of a house. Cross and turn right along a drive to reach a T-junction. Turn left to reach a road. Cross and continue along a byway opposite Boars Hole Farm. Pass between farm buildings and go ahead along the farm track. When the track bends sharp left, turn right, through a gate, and go along the field edge towards a white house. Go through a gate and along an enclosed path to reach a junction.

Here, bear right and follow the direction of blue arrow waymarkers. Go between two wooden posts and continue along a bridleway into Fence Wood. At the far end of a Christmas tree plantation, on the left, turn left along a track. At a cross-tracks, go straight across along an ascending path. Just past a pond on the right, turn right and, after 100 yards, turn left through conifers. At the next T-junction, turn right, uphill, to reach a seat on the left. Here, turn left and follow a track, which passes to the left of a house within **Grimsbury Castle**, to reach a road. Turn right along the road to reach a road junction. Turn left, downhill, and follow the road to a T-junction. Turn left to return to the Village Hall in **Hermitage**.

POINTS OF INTEREST:

St Bartholomew's Church, Oare – The poet John Betjeman once described this church as *A Victorian Gem set in the Berkshire Countryside.*

Grimsbury Castle – The house, with its 18th century battlemented tower, is built on the site of an ancient Iron Age fort, which stretches over the road you reach.

Hermitage – The novelist D H Lawrence once lived in a small cottage in the village.

REFRESHMENTS:

The White Horse, Hermitage.

Walk 79   **HAMPSTEAD NORREYS**   5$\frac{1}{2}$m (9km)

Maps: OS Sheets Landranger 174; Pathfinder 1171.

A pleasant walk in the area of the Berkshire Downs. There are a few short ascents and descents, but nothing strenuous, and some good views.

Start: At 531763, the White Hart Inn, Hampstead Norreys.

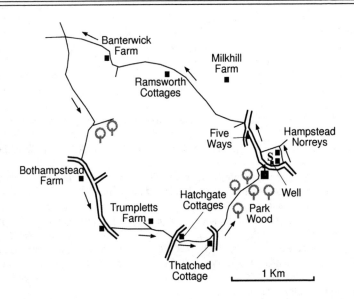

Facing the inn, take the track to the right. Fork right of some farm buildings and, after 100 yards, turn left across a field. Go through a gap and along a drive to reach a road. Turn right and follow the road to a T-junction. There is a house called Five Ways on the left. Just before a grass triangle, turn left. Cross the road, with care, and go up the track opposite (signed for Oak House Farm Mill). After 20 yards, fork right up a bridleway. Go over a rise: as you descend the other side, Milkhill Farm is on your right. The track bends left and passes Ramsworth Cottages, on the left: continue along the track to reach Banterwick Farm. Ignore a turning on the left, just before the farm, and continue ahead, bearing right of a barn. About 50 yards beyond the barn, just before an entrance into a field, turn left along a field edge, walking with a hedge on

152

your right. At the far corner, go through a gap and turn left at the cross-tracks. Now follow this green lane, which emerges from the trees and continues up the left edge of a field.

At a track junction, in the far field corner, turn right along a track which bends left, following it downhill to reach a road. Carry straight on along the road, passing Bothampstead Farm on the right, to reach a junction with a road on the left. Go straight on and, about 700 yards beyond the junction, just after some barns on the right, turn left along a bridleway. Bear right across the middle of two fields, heading towards Trumpletts Farm. Pass to the right of a barn, then go across the yard to reach a lane. Turn right and follow the lane down to reach a road at Hatchgate Cottages. Bear right across the road and take the footpath just to the right of the cottages. The path crosses a disused railway and continues up the left edge of a field. At the hedge corner, on the left, carry on across the field and, at the far side, continue along the edge of a wood. At the next corner, bear right, through a gap, to reach a minor road, with a thatched cottage on your right.

Turn left down the road and, after 30 yards, turn right up a wide track. At a junction, fork right to reach another junction. Fork left and, after 15 yards, fork left again to join a wide track through Park Wood. At a clearing on the right, continue straight on to reach a cross-tracks with a signpost on the left. Turn left down a bridleway. On emerging from the trees, with a house opposite, turn left, passing a graveyard on the left. After 50 yards, turn right along the edge of the churchyard, passing to the left of **St Mary's Church** to reach a road. Turn right and follow the road through **Hampstead Norreys**. About 50 yards after passing the **village well**, on the left, you will arrive back at the White Hart Inn.

POINTS OF INTEREST:

St Mary's Church — Look in the churchyard for the tomb of the Lowsley family. It is a stepped pyramid of cast iron made, in 1855, from disused farm implements.

Hampstead Norreys — Since being recorded in the Doomsday Book, the village has had many names: In the 13th century it was Hamstede-Sifrewast; in 1367 it was Hampstead Ferrers. It obtained its current name in 1450, when it became part of the Norreys estate.

Village Well — One of the few remaining wells in Berkshire, it was given to the village by Harry Weber, in 1903.

REFRESHMENTS:

The White Hart Inn, Hampstead Norreys.

Walk 80   **BURFORD**   5$^1/_2$m (8$^3/_4$km)

Maps: OS Sheets Landranger 163; Pathfinder 1091.

A pleasant walk from Burford, partly alongside the River Windrush to Widford with its interesting church.

Start: At 253122, the car park near Burford Church.

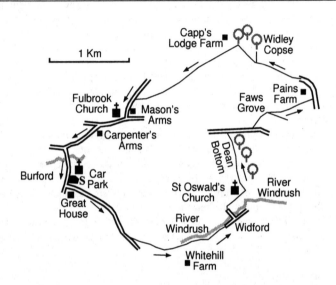

Leave the car park, through the main entrance, and turn left, uphill, through **Burford**. At the road junction, with the Royal Oak Inn just opposite, turn left. Follow the road for $^1/_2$ mile, then look for a footpath signed 'Widford 1' on the left. Cross and bear right towards the River Windrush. With the tranquil river on your left, follow the waymarked path to the village of Widford, passing Whitehill Farm on the right. On reaching a road, bear left for 200 yards to reach a road junction with Widford Mill Farm on the corner. Turn left down a 'No Through Road'. Cross the river and, after 120 yards, turn right over a cattle grid on to a farm track signed 'Swinbrook 1'. Soon, on the hill to your left, you will see **St Oswald's Church**.

Continue along the track to reach a second cattle grid. Cross and immediately swing left towards a small wood. Go through a gate and, keeping the wood on your right, follow a path up Dean Bottom, ascending gradually to reach a stile on to a road. Turn right, uphill, and, after 350 yards, turn left along a hedge-lined track, following it downhill to reach a gate and path junction. Go through the gate and continue to follow the main track, uphill, in the direction of the blue arrow waymarker. The track swings left, passing a corner of Faws Grove. There is a good view from here. Continue ahead, descending gradually to cross a stile by a gate. Carry on downhill along a stony track to reach a minor road at a bend.

Turn left, following the road, which ascends fairly steeply, past Pains Farm and on past Pains Farm Cottages. When the metalled surface ends, carry on along the gravelled track to reach a track junction just before Widley Copse. Continue straight ahead into the wood. At the far side, near a metal railing on the right, turn left across the middle of a field. There is another good view from here. At the far side, go through a gap in the wall/hedge, and continue across the next field.

Go through another gap in the far hedge, then bear right, descending gradually across the next field, heading towards the distant church steeple you can see in the valley. At the far side, turn right along the edge of the field to reach a road. Turn left into Fulbrook. Go past the Mason's Arms, on the left, and follow the road around a right-hand bend. Fulbrook Church is on the right. Continue past the Carpenter's Arms to reach a mini-roundabout. Turn left, with care, along the A361 and go over the River Windrush. After 150 yards, just past Mrs Bumbles (a shop), turn left into Church Lane. Follow the road as it bends right, then left, back to the car park.

POINTS OF INTEREST:
Burford – This attractive Cotswold village celebrated its 900th anniversary in 1990. It was once a flourishing market town dealing in wool and saddle making. Nowadays it is a tourist attraction. The 'Great House', passed early in the walk, was built in 1685. The church, Norman in origin, had its fine spire built in the 15th century. During the Civil War, in 1649, a group of Cromwellian mutineers were held captive in the church.
St Oswald's Church, Widford – This 12th-century church became disused in 1859, but was restored in 1904. It has some 14th-century wall paintings. Fragments of a Roman mosaic floor indicate that it could have been built on a Roman site. The rural setting adds to the peace and tranquillity of the church.

REFRESHMENTS:
The Mason's Arms, Fulbrook.
The Carpenter's Arms, Fulbrook.
There are a number of possibilities in Burford.

Maps: OS Sheets Landranger 174; Pathfinder 1186 and 1187.

A pleasant walk through Hamstead Park and along the Kennet and Avon Canal, returning via farm tracks and paths.

Start: At 420653, the Village Hall car park, Park Lane, Hamstead Marshal.

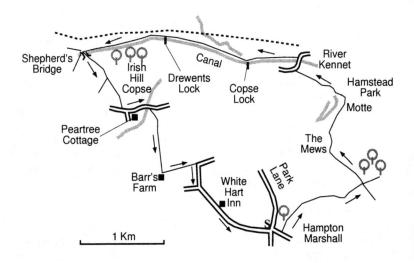

From the car park, turn right along Park Lane to reach a T-junction. Turn left for 100 yards, then turn left again over a stile next to a gate. With Ashtree Plantation on your left, proceed along a farm track. Where the track bends left, go over a stile on the right and along the left edge of a field. At the far corner, continue along a track through some trees. It can be boggy here. Go over a stile and up the left edge of two fields, with a fence and wood on your left. When the fence bends left, bear left and go up through the trees to reach a broken stile. Go over and head across the field beyond, passing between two trees, to reach a gravelled drive in Hamstead Park. Here turn left towards 'The Mews'. About 100 yards before the entrance to 'The Mews', look for a waymarker post on the right. Here, bear right along a narrow path to reach the right-hand corner of a hedged enclosure. Now, keeping the hedge on your left, continue ahead to reach a gate. Go through and head uphill to reach a drive.

Continue along the drive to reach a junction of drives. Carry straight on, downhill, noting the lakes over to your left. Just before the track bends left, there is a motte (old castle mound) on your right. Follow the drive around and over a cattle grid, continuing along it to reach a road. Turn right, passing Hampstead Mill, then crossing the River Kennet. Go over the Canal Bridge and immediately turn left along the tow-path. With the canal on your left, you now have a pleasant stretch of easy walking, watching the narrow boats go through Copse Lock and Drewent's Lock as you pass. At Shepherd's Bridge you leave the tow-path: bear right just before the bridge, heading towards a gate, then turn left over the canal bridge. After 10 yards, go over a stile on the left, then bear right, steeply, up a field. At the top, go through a gate, then ahead along a track which bends to the right. At the next gate (where there is a junction of footpaths), continue straight on, heading towards a stile next to a lone tree.

Go over the stile and bear left across the field beyond, heading for a line of old trees, to reach a stile in the bottom hedge. Go over the stile and turn left along a road. Pass Old Road, on the right, and, about 40 yards after passing some white railings (marking a bridge over a stream), turn right over a stile and go along a track enclosed by fences. Just before Barr's Farm, turn left and, after 40 yards, turn right over a stile in the fence. Bear left and cross the field beyond to reach the left-hand corner of a hedge. Here, bear sharp left across the same field, heading towards the far left corner of the field, where there is a stile. Cross the stile and turn right along a road to reach a road junction. Turn left and follow the road, passing the White Hart Inn on the left. Continue uphill to reach a road junction at Ash Tree Corner. Turn left along Park Lane: the car park is on the left about 120 yards further on.

POINTS OF INTEREST:

Hamstead Park – This was once a manor of some importance. When Henry I came to the throne in 1100, the manor became the official residence of the Marshall of the Crown. A second house was built, but this burnt down in 1718. Ironically, the then owner, Sir William Craven, had been noted for his work in fighting the great fire of London. The Cravens built a third house, but had to sell the 700 acre estate in 1984. The current house is used as a nursing home, now called 'The Mews'.

REFRESHMENTS:

The White Hart Inn, Hamstead Marshal. The inn is not open on Sundays. Then, walkers will need to travel to Kintbury, about 2 miles to the west.

Walk 82   **MIDDLE BARTON** $5^3/_4$m ($9^1/_4$km)
Maps: OS Sheets Landranger 164; Pathfinder 1069.

A pleasant walk in gently undulating country, along tracks and green lanes. Some of the hedgerows passed on the walk are estimated to be 800 years old.

Start: At 438257, in Mill Lane, just off the B4030, near the ford.

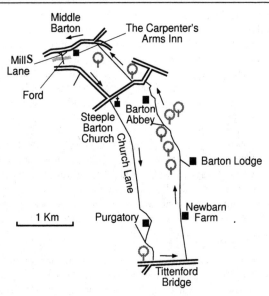

Go down Mill Lane, **Middle Barton**, crossing the ford using the tarmac path on the left. On the other side, fork left, uphill, through barriers, to reach a road (Church Lane). Turn left, passing a school on the left. Go over a crossing track and, at a cross-roads, carry straight on to reach St Mary's Church, **Steeple Barton**, on the left. Continue along the lane which soon becomes a pleasant green track. On reaching an open field, bear left along the field edge. Go through a gate on the left and bear diagonally right across the next field to reach a gate in the opposite corner. Go through and bear right along the field edge.

When the hedge and fence on the right ends, continue ahead across a narrow field. On your right is a fairly large farm. This area is marked on the map as 'Purgatory', and it probably is in the depths of Winter. At the far left corner of the field you will join a crossing track: turn left through a gate and follow the track beyond as it bends left, then right, following the field edge to reach a road. Turn left over Tittenford Bridge, following the road uphill for 600 yards to reach a bridleway crossing. Here, turn left along a broad track.

Follow the track to Newbarn Farm. Go between the farm, on the right, and a barn, on the left, and continue along the track. Soon after dropping down through some trees the track joins a metalled lane coming in from the right. Maintain direction along the lane. Where the lane turns right into Barton Lodge, continue straight on down a narrower track, which, further down, bends to the left. Ignore a track going off to the left, continuing to reach a gate. Go through and cross the park land beyond.

Opposite a stone built cricket pavilion on the right, if you look left you can just see the top part of **Barton Abbey**. Keep on along the main track to reach a gate. Go through and continue to reach a drive. Turn right, uphill, to reach a road. Turn left along the road, which bends right, then left, downhill. Just after passing a house on the right, turn right up the house drive, and, after 10 yards, bear left along a track. Go through a gate and across a field to reach the corner of a copse on the left.

Continue along the field edge, keeping the copse on your left. Go through a gate on the left, and down through the copse. On emerging, cross a plank bridge, and go across a field to reach a gate just left of the far right-hand corner, near a house. Go between houses to reach a road. Go past Rayford Lane, on the left, continuing along the pavement into Middle Barton. Go past the Carpenter's Arms Inn, on the left, and, after 75 yards, turn left down a narrow lane (Jacob's Yard). Go past a barrier and, after 5 yards, turn right to follow a lane to Mill Lane, emerging with the ford on your left.

POINTS OF INTEREST:

Middle and Steeple Barton – The word 'Barton' means an outlying farm. The Bartons consist of three villages, the other one being Westcote. Steeple Barton once supplied the food for the Royal manor at Woodstock. It is thought that Middle Barton was populated by people fleeing the Black Death which had ravaged Steeple Barton. A 1923 magazine reported Steeple Barton as being 'the healthiest village for many a mile'.

Barton Abbey – This is simply a large, mainly Victorian, house. It has never been an abbey, being named by the Halls, a family of brewers.

REFRESHMENTS:

The Carpenter's Arms, Middle Barton.

Walk 83   **WATLINGTON HILL**   6m (9$\frac{1}{2}$km)

Maps: OS Sheets Landranger 175 and 165; Explorer 3.

A walk providing fine views across the Oxford plain and across to the Chiltern beech woods.

Start: At 709935, the National Trust car park on Watlington Hill.

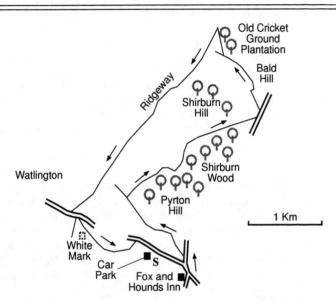

Leave through the car park's main entrance and turn right along the road to reach a road junction. Turn left for 40 yards, then go left over a stile and along the left edge of a field beyond to reach another stile. Cross the field beyond, bearing slightly right, away from the left-hand hedge and going through some trees to reach a stile at the far side. Cross and turn left down a track. At the bottom, walk past a house and a woodyard on the left, and, just before the scrub on the right ends, turn right along a track, passing a chain barrier. Keep to the main track as it skirts the lower slopes of Pyrton Hill, then, where the track turns right, veer left along a narrow path, walking with a wire fence on your left. The path bends right but stays at the woodland edge: where the path rejoins the wider track, turn left to follow the lower track. As the track starts to ascend, look for a narrow path on the left. Now, still keeping to the lower edge, the

160

path eventually emerges on to open ground at the bottom of Shirburn Hill. The path now bends right and ascends Shirburn Hill. Before reaching the top, turn around to admire the view. At the top, go over a crossing track and the stile opposite, and cross a field to reach a stile in the far left corner. Go over and turn left along a road for 40 yards, then turn left down a path just to the left of an Ashton Rowant Nature Reserve sign-board. A footpath sign states 'Lewknor $1^1/_2$'.

The path descends quite steeply: go over a stile and continue along the path, which now runs just to the left of the Nature Reserve boundary fence. The ground to your right is called Bald Hill and is a haven for rabbits. Continue to descend gradually to reach **Old Cricket Ground Plantation** on the right. Now look for a stile on the right, cross it and follow the path beyond through a wood. On emerging from the wood, cross a field to reach the wide Ridgeway track. Turn left along the Ridgeway, following it for the next 2 miles (at one point crossing the metalled Oxfordshire Way) to reach a road near the bottom of Watlington Hill. Cross, with care, and turn left, uphill, for 30 yards, then bear right up a narrow path which soon opens out. Do not go over a stile on the right: instead, continue ahead, through a swing gate, and, after 20 yards, turn left and ascend **Watlington Hill**, keeping just to the left of a large white chalk mark cut into the hillside.

The ascent here is quite steep, but the views from the top are well worth the effort. At the top, after you have got your breath back, bear left along the ridge, following a well-defined path. You can see much of the area covered on the walk from here. When you reach a small copse, go through a gate and walk ahead to reach the road again. Turn right along the path alongside the road, go up some steps, and, finally, go up a grassy bank to return to the car park.

POINTS OF INTEREST:
Old Cricket Ground Plantation – This small section of woodland is so named because its ownership was once the prize in a local cricket match.
Watlington Hill – A large area of chalk down and copse, the hill was given to the National Trust in 1941 by the 3rd Viscount and Viscountess Esher. It rises to over 700 feet. The white mark cut into the hillside is said to represent the outline of a church steeple. Best seen from a distance, north of Watlington, it gives the impression that the church which nestles below the hill has a large spire.

REFRESHMENTS:
The Fox and Hounds Inn, Christmas Common.
There are also possibilities in Watlington.

Walk 84   WALBURY HILL AND COOMBE GIBBET   6m (9¹/₂km)

Maps: OS Sheets Landranger 174; Pathfinder 1186.

A visit to an old iron age fort and the one time site of executions should not deter you from some fine panoramic views.

Start: At 378638, the Crown and Garter Inn, Inkpen Common.

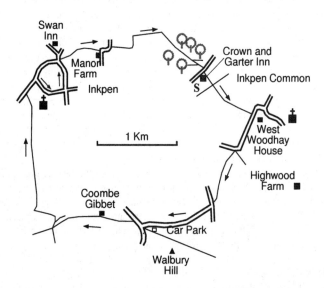

If you use the inn car park, please check with the landlord beforehand. From the car park at the rear of the inn, turn right along a broad lane. Ignore footpaths to both left and right, following the lane to reach a road. Turn right and follow the road to reach a sharp right-hand bend. Here, go straight ahead along a footpath just to the left of a copse. Follow the path across fields to reach a road at a road junction. Take the road on the right which ascends the hill quite steeply to reach another road junction at the top of the ridge. **Walbury Hill**, and a small car park, are on the left. There is an information board with details about the area.

At the road junction, turn right up a bridleway (Test Way), heading towards the **Long Barrow** and **Coombe Gibbet**, which you can see on the hill. There are some excellent views from the ridge. Go past the gibbet, walking for about another ¹/₂ mile to reach a track junction. Here, go ahead for 30 yards, then turn right through a gate. Veer right across the hillside to pass to the left of a small pond. After another 30 yards, turn left down a shallow gully which bends left and descends the hillside, quite steeply, to reach a gate at the bottom. Go through and follow a path, and then a track, to reach a road. Turn right to reach a road junction, turning right again to go uphill, passing Inkpen Church on the right. At a crossroads, turn left and follow the road down to a T-junction. Turn right and, after 20 yards, turn right again to go along the short drive of Ingebrooke House. Now keep to the left to pick up a path between hedges. The path bends left, then right, along a field edge. Cross a wooden footbridge and the boggy ground beyond to reach a fence on the left. Turn right, go over two stiles and then turn right towards Manor Farm. Just before the farm, turn left through a gate and follow a path, keeping to the left of the farm, to reach another gate and a road. Go ahead, along the road and, just after a left-hand bend, go over a stile on the right. Bear left across a field (following the direction of the footpath sign), heading towards a chalet-style bungalow. Go over a stile on the left, near a tree and fence corner, and continue along the right-hand edge of the house grounds, walking with the fence on your right. When the fence ends, bear right up a bank. Go to the right of a laurel bush and climb to a squeeze stile in the fence.

Go through and turn left along a drive which becomes metalled. Continue past stables, on the right, and go up a grassy track to a T-junction. Turn right along a path through a wood. Go over a crossing path and continue between fields to reach a road. Bear right across the road and go over a stile to the right of a gate. Follow the path beyond through a wood, going over two streams and a crossing path between them. At the next path junction, with a stone on the right, go straight on to reach a road, passing to the left of a thatched house. Cross the road, with care, and follow the broad track opposite. After 30 yards, turn right into the inn car park.

POINTS OF INTEREST:
Walbury Hill – At 974 feet this is the highest chalk hill in England.
Long Barrow – Details about the barrow and Walbury Hill Iron Age Camp are given on the information board in the car park, as mentioned in the text.
Coombe Gibbet – The gibbet stands on the barrow. It is in good order and ready for use. Originally erected in 1676 for the hanging of a man and woman for murder, the gibbet you see now is the third to stand here.

REFRESHMENTS:
The Crown and Garter Inn, Inkpen Common.
The Swan Inn, Lower Green.

Walk 85   **Dorchester**   6m (9$^1/_2$km)

Maps: OS Sheets Landranger 174; Pathfinder 1136.

The ancient town of Dorchester, a large fortification known as Dyke Hills, the site of an iron age fort, and a walk along the Thames all feature on this walk.

Start: At 578941, the car park in Bridge End, Dorchester.

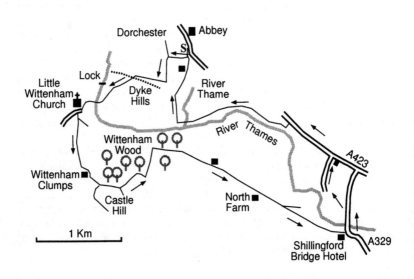

From the car park, go down Bridge End, passing St Birinus' Roman Catholic Chapel on the left. Just past the Chequers Inn, on the right, turn right along Walling Lane. Where the lane bends right, near some allotments, turn left along an enclosed footpath, signed 'Days Lock $^3/_4$', to reach a field. Go along the left edge to reach the impressive **Dyke Hills** earthworks. Turn right, go over at a cross-tracks and then go along a fenced track which bends left towards the River Thames. Where the track ends. go through a gate and bear left across a field to Day's Lock footbridge. Cross this and two smaller bridges, and bear left along a lane to reach St Peter's Church, Little Wittenham, on your right. Turn left, through a gate, into the Little Wittenham Nature Reserve, and bear right across a field. Go through a gate and ascend Round Hill to reach a clump of trees (**Wittenham Clumps**), where there is a small toposcope. Turn left along the edge of the clump, keeping the trees to your right. At the corner, go straight ahead, towards Castle Hill, heading down the grassy slope towards a gate. Pass the gate, on your left, and go over a stile. Go down steps, then up the slope of the Iron Age hillfort's ramparts. Continue ahead to reach a clump of trees, turn left along a path just inside the clump. When you emerge, just on your right stands a 'Poem Tree'. Stop and peruse its verse. Now, from the tree, bear left for 100 yards and descend the rampart to reach a stile.

Cross and follow a path, downhill, along the left edge of a field, continuing down the field to reach a gate just to the right of the bottom corner. Turn left through the gate and walk ahead. going over at a cross-tracks in the Nature Reserve. Follow a broad track down to a barrier. Go past the barrier and, after 10 yards, turn right along a bridleway. Leave the wood and go over a stream, continuing along a field edge. Go past North Farm, to your right, and walk along a lane to reach the A329 at Shillingford Bridge. Turn left, with care, over the bridge, and, after 50 yards, turn left along a Private Road (signed for the Thames Path). At the sign for 'Hazeldene/High Trees', bear right through a kissing gate and go along an enclosed path. At the end of the wall of Shillingford Court, on the left, turn left past a barrier. Go around a second barrier and turn right along Wharf Road to reach the A423. Turn left, with care, to reach the Dorchester road sign. Now go through the gate on the left to reach the river. Turn right and follow the river-bank, with the river on your left, to reach a bridge over the River Thame.

Cross and turn right along a footpath, heading across fields towards **Dorchester**. Cross several stiles, passing Dyke Hills again (on your left) to reach a lane. Continue ahead to reach a road at the Chequers Inn. Now carry straight on to return to the car park. Dorchester Abbey is just beyond.

POINTS OF INTEREST:

Dyke Hills – These ancient fortifications, which pre-date the Romans, were built to defend Dorchester.

Wittenham Clumps – The name is given to the two hills, Round Hill and Castle Hill. The latter is the site of a large hillfort.

Dorchester – Dating back approximately 5.000 years, the town has a great deal of interest. The Abbey was built in 634AD by Bishop Birinus and is well worth a visit.

REFRESHMENTS:

The Shillingford Bridge Hotel, Shillingford.
There are also ample opportunities in Dorchester.

Walk 86   UFFINGTON WHITE HORSE   6m (9¹/₂km)

Maps: OS Sheets Landranger 174; Pathfinder 1154.

This walk visits two very ancient sites and also includes a pleasant ridge walk and a descent into the valley.

Start: At 293865, Woolstone Hill car park.

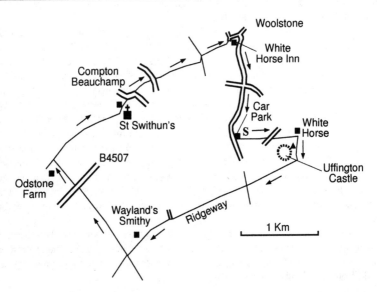

With your back to the road, cross the car park and go through the gate on the other side. Bear right, uphill, heading for the top of the **Uffington White Horse**, which can be clearly seen on the hillside. Go over a minor road and continue until you are standing just above the horse, where there is an information board. From here, bear sharp right, uphill, aiming for the left edge of Uffington Castle, where there is a trig. point. There are excellent views from here.

From the trig. point, with the ancient fort on your right, go ahead for 100 yards to reach a gate and the Ridgeway path. Turn right, downhill, and follow the Ridgeway for 1¹/₂ miles to reach **Wayland's Smithy**, on the right. The route and site are well signposted. On leaving the site, turn right for 200 yards, to reach a cross-tracks. Here, turn right and follow a track, which, level at first, soon descends Odstone Hill to reach the B4507. Cross the road, with care, and continue down the farm track opposite to reach Odstone Farm, on the left. Keep to the right as you pass the farm to reach a gate. Go through and turn right through a second, larger, gate. Now go along the right edge of a field, cross a stile and a footbridge and continue along the edges of the next two fields. At the far side of the second field, go through a gap in the hedge and cross the middle of the next field to reach a wooden swing gate, just to the left of a copse. Go through the gate and bear left across the field beyond.

In the opposite field corner, go through a gap and down the right edge of the field beyond. **St Swithun's Church** is now on your right. Near the entrance to the churchyard, go through a gate and turn left, passing a barn on the left, noting the clock on its roof. Continue down the church drive to reach a road. The entrance to Compton Beauchamp House is on the right.

Continue straight on and, where the road swings right, uphill, go through a gate and walk ahead to reach another gate just to the left of a house. Go through and continue along the right edges of two fields, with a small wood on your right, to reach a road. Bear left across the road and go over the stile opposite. Continue ahead to reach another stile. Go over this and a footbridge, following the path beyond through a narrow belt of trees. At the far side, cross a small bridge and go along the left edge of the field beyond.

At the far corner, cross another small bridge and follow a faint, winding path through some scrub to reach a crossing track (Hardwell Lane). Turn left for 100 yards, then turn right over a stile and go along the right edge of a field. Go through a gate and cross the next field to reach a stile on to a road. Go ahead, along the road, to reach the White Horse Inn on the right. At the road junction beyond, turn right and follow a road uphill. Cross the B4507, with care, and continue up the road opposite to return to the car park, which will be on your left.

POINTS OF INTEREST:
Uffington White Horse – The origin of this chalk figure is unknown. Even its age is in dispute. The figure is 365 ft long and 130 ft tall.
Wayland's Smithy – This is a Neolithic burial chamber dated between 3500BC and 3000BC. A number of skeletons were found during excavations.
St Swithun's Church – The church is worth a visit to see the beautiful chancel wall paintings.

REFRESHMENTS:
The White Horse Inn, Woolstone.

Walk 87   **EAST ADDERBURY**   6m (9¹/₂km)

Maps: OS Sheets Landranger 151; Pathfinder 1045.

A fairly level walk, visiting Adderbury Lake and including a long stretch along the Oxford Canal tow-path.

Start: At 480356, along the 'No Through Road', near the entrance to East House, East Adderbury.

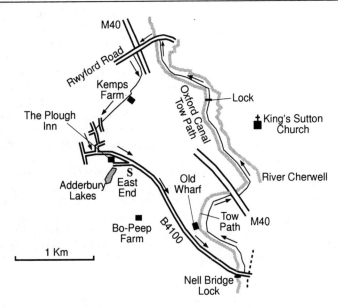

Go up the 'No Through Road' and fork right along a metalled footpath, passing a cottage called Old Mark's on the right. Continue ahead along Longwall to reach a wooden gate in the wall on the left. Go through this to visit **Adderbury Lakes**. Take the path past the upper lake, on the left, then go left over a footbridge to walk round the lower lake, on the right. Retrace your steps back to the wooden gate and turn right along Longwall to reach the B4100.

Turn right along the B4100, keeping to the verge, to pass Katherine House Hospice, and Bo-Peep Farm on the right. Cross the road, with care, and continue along the verge on the other side, passing the entrance to Banbury Business Park on the left. Just past Riyes Cottage, on the left, bear left along a minor road, which runs parallel to the B4100, to reach Nell Bridge. Cross the bridge and turn left down to the Oxford Canal tow-path.

Continue along the tow-path, which runs between the canal on the left and the River Cherwell on the right. Further on, the tow-path bends right and passes under the M40 motorway. Shortly after, the tow-path bends left again to run almost parallel with the motorway, but not in sight of it. Over to your right you can see the steeple of King's Sutton Church, which is in Northamptonshire. On reaching King's Sutton Lock, go up the steps beside the Lock Cottage and continue ahead.

On reaching the next stone built bridge, go under, then immediately turn right up to a road. Turn right over the canal, then go over the M40 motorway. Immediately after crossing the M40, turn left over the crash barrier, then go over a stile, signed for 'Adderbury 1'. Go along the left edge of a field, cross a stile in the corner and bear right up the next field, heading towards the right-hand corner of Kemp's Farm. Cross a stile and continue up to the corner of the farm buildings.

Go over a barrier stile by a barn, and turn left along the edge of a field to reach a swing gate. Go through and turn right along the farm drive to reach a road. Turn left along the road and, just after it bends right, turn left to follow a road around to the right to reach a T-junction. Turn left for 30 yards to reach another T-junction (with the B4100). Cross, with care, and turn left. Walk past the Plough Inn, **Adderbury**, on the right, soon reaching the entrance to East End House, also on the right.

POINTS OF INTEREST:

Adderbury Lakes – The well-known 18th-century landscape designer, Capability Brown, laid out these lakes. The lakes, and the various trees and flowers in the surrounding area, are a haven for wildlife.

Adderbury – The village of Adderbury was known as Eadburg in the Doomsday Book. Adderbury House has housed troops from wars as far apart as the Civil War and the Second World War. During the Civil War, Prince Rupert of the Rhine and the 1st Earl of Rochester were Royalist commanders there.

REFRESHMENTS:
The Plough Inn, Adderbury.
There are other possibilities in the centre of the village.

Walk 88   ENSTONE   6m (9¹/₂km)

Maps: OS Sheets Landranger 164; Pathfinder 1068.

A pleasant walk along tracks and paths, skirting woodland to the south of the village of Enstone. There are some undulations but most of the walk is fairly level.

Start: At 376242, Enstone Post Office.

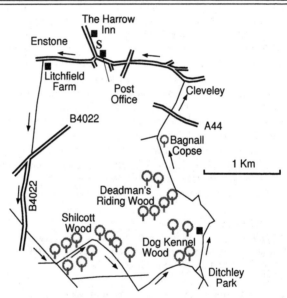

With your back to the Post Office, cross the A44, with care, and go up Fulwell Road opposite. After 100 yards, turn right along the Lidstone road. After 700 yards, at a sign for Litchfield Farm and Dower House, turn left up a bridleway, passing the farm on the left. Continue along the track, with a hedge on the right at first, then going across open fields, to reach the B4022. Cross, with care, and turn right along the grass verge to reach a road junction.

Continue along the B4022 for approximately ¹/₂ mile, then, at a dip in the road, turn left up a hedge-enclosed path, following a line of telegraph wires. Continue along the edge of Shilcott Wood, on the left, to reach a metalled track joining from the right.

Here, turn left, then, after 20 yards, turn left through a gate into the wood. Follow a track through the wood to reach a fairly wide clearing. Here, turn right to reach the corner of the wood, on the right.

Continue straight ahead on a clear path across the field. At the far side, go through a gap in the hedge, then turn left along a farm track. Keep to the track when it bends right. You now have a wooden fence on your left, and a wood on your right. You will join a drive coming in from the left: bear right, then take the next turning on the left and follow this track down to a T-junction. Turn left, passing a stone cottage on the right. Now ignore a turning on the right, continuing straight on. Over to your left at this point is Dog Kennel Wood.

Carry on past a house on the left, continuing up the track to reach a black barn. Turn left along a field edge, walking with a hedge on your right, passing to the right of some old brick buildings. Immediately turn left to reach Deadman's Riding Wood, turning right along the wood's edge. There are some good views from here. When the wood ends, on the left, go through a gap and walk along the edge of a field.

At the field corner, go through the hedge and continue down the left edge of the next field. At the next corner, at the bottom of a small valley, bear diagonally right up the field, passing to the left of Bagnall Copse. At the top of the field, go through a gap to reach the A44. Cross the road, with great care, and continue along the bridleway opposite, following it through a narrow strip of woodland. At the far side, continue along a track to reach a road at Cleveley.

Turn left, passing a telephone kiosk, and follow the broad back towards **Enstone**. On reaching a crossroads, go straight across, following Cleveley Road opposite. At the next T-junction, turn right along the A44, following it back to Enstone Post Office, which will be on your right.

POINTS OF INTEREST:
Enstone – Enstone actually consists of two villages, Church Enstone and Neat Enstone, situated either sides of the Glyme valley. The village of Neat Enstone, from which you start the walk, has some fine stone-built houses. Enstone was built around a triangle of ancient turnpike roads (now the B4022, the B4030 and the A44) and once had six coaching inns.

REFRESHMENTS:
The Harrow Inn, Enstone.

Walk 89   **BARKHAM**   6m (9$^{1}/_{2}$km)

Maps: OS Sheets Landranger 175; Pathfinder 1188.

A pleasant walk across fields, along tracks and through woodland, in an area on the western edge of what was once part of Windsor Great Forest.

Start: At 783664, the Barkham Church Hall car park.

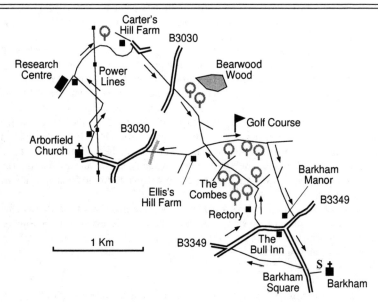

Leave the car park and turn right to reach a road junction. Cross and turn right. After 50 yards, turn left along enclosed path, walking with a fence on your right. Go over a stile and continue along the left edge of four fields. In the fourth field, just after passing a house on the left, cross a stile, on the left, on to a drive. Turn right to reach the B3349. Cross, with care, and turn right along the road. About 75 yards after crossing a bridge, turn left along a signed bridleway. When the track turns left to the Old Rectory, continue ahead over a wooden barrier, then follow the narrowing path up through woodland. Go past a house on the left, continuing along the path as it bends to the right and ascends more steeply. Near the top, look for two white arrows on a tree to your left: take the left-hand fork to reach a path junction. Turn left and follow

172

a path down a dip, across a wooden bridge, then up the steps on the other side. Go ahead for 20 yards, then bear right, following the faded white arrows on the trees. The path bends left, then right over an earth bridge to reach a cross-paths. Here, turn left, go over a wooden bridge and continue to reach a cross-tracks. Go straight ahead. Shortly, you will have a field and fence on your left: go through a zig-zag fence and up the steep narrow path beyond to reach a wide track junction. Turn left, passing the entrance to Ellis's Hill Farm, on the left, and, after a further 20 yards, bear right along a wide track. Go past a house on the left and continue along the track. Cross a bridge and continue to reach the B3030. Turn left and follow the road, with care, to reach a road junction. Bear right along Church Lane (signed 'Arborfield Church') and, after 250 yards, bear right along a byway signed 'To Monks Cottage only'. Go past the Old Reading Room, and continue past Monks Cottage, both on the left. After passing under power lines, the track bends left towards a red brick house.

At the track junction just beyond the house, turn right and follow a track to Carter's Hill Farm, on your left. Cross a footbridge, then go up past Tudor House Aquatic Garden, on the left, to reach a minor road. Turn right, but, after 100 yards, bear right along a track, following it to reach the B3030 again. Cross, with care, and continue up the track opposite, going through woodland. On reaching a wide track junction at the top, turn left. Follow the track for 600 yards. On your left, in the small valley you have just come out of, you may be able to see part of Bear Wood Lake. On your right are The Coombes, which you came through earlier on the walk. When the woodland on the right ends, turn right over a barrier. Now, ignoring all paths and tracks going off to both left and right, continue down Barkham Hill to reach the B3349. **Barkham Manor** is on your right, just before you reach the road. At the road, turn right, then, after 200 yards, cross, with care, and go up the road opposite. The Bull Inn is on your right. After 600 yards, turn left and follow a road back to **Barkham Church**.

POINTS OF INTEREST:

Barkham Manor – The Ball family, reputed ancestors of George Washington, once lived in Barkham Manor. A Plane Orientalis tree, thought to be 400-500 years old stands at the front of the house.

Barkham Church – The present church dates from 1862, built partly from materials used in an earlier church. The chalice dates from the reign of Charles I.

REFRESHMENTS:
The Bull Inn, Barkham.

Walks 90 & 91   **ABINGDON**   6m (9$\frac{1}{2}$km)
                                              or 9$\frac{1}{2}$m (15$\frac{1}{4}$km)

Maps: OS Sheets Landranger 164; Pathfinder 1136.
A pleasant walk beside the River Thames/Isis.
Start: At 499968, the car park on the south side of Abingdon
Bridge.

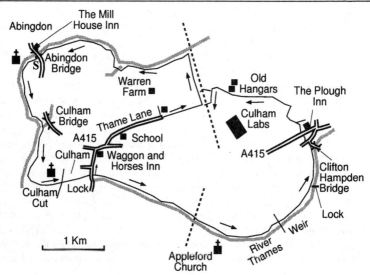

From the car park, head towards the river and turn left along the tow-path. The town
of **Abingdon** is on the opposite side. Soon, in the distance, you will be able to see the
cooling towers of Didcot Power Station. Cross a bridge and, on your left, is the
picturesque setting of Culham Road Bridge. Continue ahead to reach Culham Cut.
Here the tow-path bends left to follow the left bank of the Cut. Over to your left you
can see the village of Culham. Go past a footbridge, on the right, leading to Sutton
Courtney, and then on past Culham Lock to reach Sutton Bridge.

    The shorter walk turns left along the road here. Go past Culham High Street, on
the left, and continue to reach the A415. The Waggon and Horses Inn is on the right-
hand corner. Cross the road, with care, and turn right. After 250 yards, turn left into
Thame Lane (signed 'European School'). Go past the school, on the right, continuing

along the lane to reach a house, on the left. Now carry straight on along a gravelled track to reach a bridge over the railway. Just before this, turn left along a footpath, keeping the railway on your right, rejoining the longer route.

The longer walk crosses the road, with care and goes over the stile opposite. Now continue along the tow-path. Over to your right you can see Didcot Power Station. In just over a mile, you pass under a railway line. Soon, to your right, you will see the village of Appleford and the **Church of St Peter and St Paul**. Continue along the tow-path, passing a weir, a farm bridge over the river, and Clifton Lock before reaching the Clifton Hampden road bridge. Here, turn left along the road, reaching a junction after 50 yards. Turn left and, after 100 yards, turn sharp right up a short gravelled track. At its end, continue along an enclosed path, which runs at the back of some gardens on the right, to reach the A415. Turn left and, after 20 yards, turn right across the road, with care, and continue along the track opposite. At the far end, go through a gap in a hedge, then along a concrete path, walking with a wire fence on your left to reach the boundary fence of Culham Laboratories. Turn right and follow the fence. Shortly after passing some old hangars, on the right, the track, and the fence, bend left. After 150 yards, bend left again, then, after a further 200 yards, near a gate, turn right to reach a railway line. Cross the bridge and immediately turn right along a path, keeping the railway on your right. The shorter route has now been rejoined.

Follow the path, beside the railway cutting, to reach the River Thames. Here, turn left along the tow-path, following the River Thames or Isis all the way back to Abingdon Bridge. Just before reaching the bridge, on the opposite bank, is the picturesque setting of the Mill House Inn. Follow the tow-path under the bridge, then turn left back to the car park.

POINTS OF INTEREST:

Abingdon – Until 1974, this was the county town of Berkshire. Its Abbey, founded in 675AD, and now a ruin, was the second most important in the country, Glastonbury being the first. The town has a great deal of interest and is well worth a visit.

Church of St Peter and St Paul, Appleford – Buried in the churchyard, in an unmarked grave, is one John Faulkener, who died in 1933 aged 104. A jockey, he rode his first race when he was 8 years old, and his last when he was 70.

REFRESHMENTS:

The Mill House Inn, Abingdon.
The Waggon and Horses Inn, Culham.
The Plough Inn, Clifton Hampden.

Walk 92   RADCOT BRIDGE   6¼m (10km)

Maps: OS Sheets Landranger 163 and 164; Pathfinder 1135 and 1115.

Starting from the oldest bridge over the River Thames, this level walk crosses meadows, then returns along the Thames tow-path.
Start: At 285994, the Radcot Bridge car park.

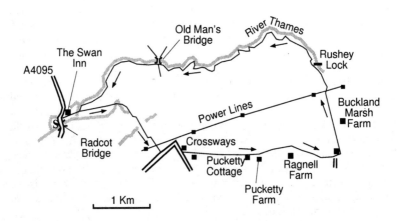

From the car park, turn right along the bank of the Thames, keeping the river on your left. Cross a wooden bridge, then bear right, away from the river, to reach a stile 20 yards to the left of a gate. Go over and continue along the edge of the field beyond, walking with a fence and a small stream on the right. Follow the stream to reach a wooden bridge in the far corner. Cross and go through a gate on the other side, then turn right along the field edge. The path tends to get overgrown here.

Go through a gate in the far corner and over another stream. After 10 yards, turn left to cross a small plank bridge over a ditch, then turn right along the right edge of a field, passing under some power cables, to reach a road. Turn left for 250 yards, then follow the road around a sharp right-hand bend. After 100 yards, just beyond a house called 'Crossways', turn left along a bridleway, signed 'Carswell Marsh 1½'. Go past Brixton Farm and Pucketty Cottage, both on the right, continuing to reach Pucketty Farm.

At the farm, go through a gate and turn left around the inner boundary of the garden. At the far side, bear left across a wooden bridge, go through a gate, and continue ahead across a field. Ragnell Farm is on the right. Go over two bridges and bear slightly right across the next field. Go over a stile at the far side and continue along a track which joins a drive coming from the left. Go through a gate and bear left along a minor road, passing some stone cottages.

After the last cottage, go through a gate and immediately turn left, to go along the side of the cottage. Continue ahead along the edge of two fields. Now, just before the corner of the second field, ignore a bridge on the left, continuing ahead to cross a bridge at the corner. Carry on along the edge of the next field and, in the far corner, turn right for 5 yards, then turn left through a gap in the hedge. Go over a stile and continue across a grassy strip to reach the bank of the River Thames.

Turn left to reach Rushey Lock. The route now follows the Thames Path back to **Radcot Bridge**, passing, on the way, **Old Man's Bridge** and Radcot Lock. As you approach Radcot Bridge, the welcoming site of the Swan Inn is seen on the opposite bank of the river. Note that the oldest bridge of the two, at Radcot, is the one furthest away from the Swan Inn.

POINTS OF INTEREST:

Radcot Bridge – This is thought to be the oldest bridge crossing the River Thames. Parts of the bridge almost certainly date from the 12th to 14th centuries. A battle was fought in the area in 1387, during the rebellion against King Richard II. The area was also involved in Civil War battles. The Thames, near Radcot Bridge, is a popular spot for anglers these days and the car park can become quite full, walkers needing to avoid the rods and the creels emerging from many of the cars.

Old Man's Bridge – An old flash weir once existed on this site, over which a right of way had been established. When the weir was dismantled and removed, the bridge was built in order that the public right of way could be maintained.

REFRESHMENTS;
The Swan Inn, Radcot Bridge.

Maps: OS Sheets Landranger 163; Pathfinder 1135.

A walk providing good views of the Berkshire Downs and a visit to a medieval barn.

Start: At 262946, the National Trust car park on Badbury Hill.

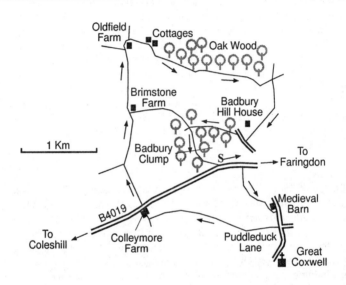

From the car park, return to the road and turn left, with care. After about 200 yards, just before a crossroads sign, turn right along a footpath, heading downhill with good views of the Berkshire Downs in the distance. At the bottom of the field turn left over a stile and bear right across the corner of a small plantation to reach a small footbridge and stile. Cross into a field and turn left to follow its edge. **Great Coxwell Barn** is immediately in front of you. Just past the barn, turn left over a stile and go between the barn and some out-buildings to reach a road. Turn right along it to reach Puddleduck Lane, on the right. To visit the 12th-century church of St Giles, continue straight ahead then return to this point.

Turn along Puddleduck Lane, walking past houses and a barn, with good views to the left. The tarmac lane soon becomes a track passing between hedgerows: continue along it, but when the hedgerows end, go through a gate and cross a field, bending slightly left with the track. A medieval ploughing system was once used in these fields. Go through two gates, close together, and then through another gate. Continue through two more gates, then turn right along a concrete track, following it through 18th-century Colleymore Farm to reach the B4019 again.

Cross, with care, and continue along the track opposite. At a T-junction, turn right and follow a track to Brimstone Farm. Go through the farmyard and walk ahead to reach Oldfield Farm. At the farm, bear left, then right, with the track, keeping the farm buildings on your right. Beyond the barns, turn right towards some stone cottages. At the cottages, bear right, through a gate, and cross a small field to reach a second gate. Go through and immediately turn left along the field edge.

On reaching a woodland edge the path bears right, cutting the field corner, to cross a small wooden bridge and stile at the corner of Oak Wood. Continue ahead, following the edge of Oak Wood for about $^3/_4$ mile. When the wood ends, turn left along a track. Go through a gateway and bear right across a field to the opposite corner. Here, turn right over a stile, then go right again (following the blue arrow) along the field edge. In the distance to your left you can see, on top of a hill, Farringdon Folly. When the hedge on the right ends, go straight ahead across the field to reach a stile.

Cross the stile and go along the left edge of the field beyond. Go through a gate and walk uphill to go through a second gate. Continue uphill across open grassland, then cross a gravel track and climb to reach a small gate in the hedge. Go through the gate and turn right along a narrow road. After 150 yards, at a road junction, turn left up a track at the edge of small wood on the right. At the field corner the path enters the wood: go straight ahead along a meandering path to reach a wide junction of tracks. Turn left, uphill, following the main track back to the car park. Just before reaching the car park, look to your left to see **Badbury Clump**.

POINTS OF INTEREST:

Great Coxwell Barn – The barn dates back to the 13th century. It was built by Cistercian monks of Beaulieu Abbey in Hampshire to keep the parish tithes paid by local farmers. It is over 150 ft long and was donated to the National Trust in 1956.

Badbury Clump – This is the site of an Iron Age fort, although finds of pottery and flints suggest that the area was inhabited even earlier.

REFRESHMENTS:

None on the route. The nearest are at Coleshill to the west, or in Farringdon to the east.

Walk 94   WATERPERRY AND WATERSTOCK   7m (11km)

Maps: OS Sheets Landranger 164; Pathfinder 1117.

A fairly level walk over the boundary into Buckinghamshire and back. It can be muddy in wet weather - as the walk title suggests.

Start: At 627064, Waterperry Gardens car park.

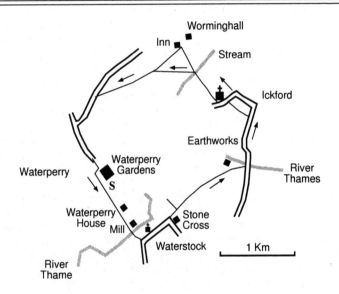

Before starting, please note the timings for the car park. From the car park, head towards the right-hand boundary of the grounds of **Waterperry House**. On reaching them, turn left until you are just opposite the house. Here, turn right through a gap and cross a ditch to reach a wide crossing track. Turn left to reach a gate. Turn left along a footpath to reach a drive. Turn right along the gravel track, passing a small lodge, to reach a bridge over the River Thame. Continue ahead, through a gate, passing the timber-framed Waterstock Mill, on the left, to reach a road.

Turn left into Waterstock, passing the **church** on your left. Ignore the Oxfordshire Way sign on the right, continuing along the road through the village. About 20 yards after a sharp right-hand bend, turn left along a track, passing a stone cross on the right. When the main track bends left, continue straight ahead along the right edge of a field, with a small wood on your right. At the first corner, where the wood ends, head straight across the field, aiming just to the right of a barn seen in the distance. Cross a stile near a lone tree, and maintain direction across the next two fields to reach a road. Turn left and follow the road to Ickford. As you enter the village, look for the Village Hall on the left. About 40 yards beyond the hall, turn left along a footpath enclosed by fences. Go over a stile, cross the field beyond, then go over two more stiles and follow another enclosed footpath to emerge on a drive, with a house on your left. Continue ahead along the drive to reach a road. Turn left to reach Ickford Church.

Go through the church gates and walk through the churchyard, keeping the church to your right. Cross a stone bridge and stile into a field and follow a yellow waymarker arrow to reach and cross a stile in the far corner. Bear right across the next field to reach a footbridge over a stream. (If you intend visiting the inn in Worminghall bear right across the field to the gate in the far corner – the inn is on the left.) Turn left to walk beside the stream, but when the stream bends left, head across the field to reach a stile on the left, just before the field corner - do not go into the field with the barn. Cross a stile/bridge and bear right across a field to another stile/bridge. Now maintain direction to meet a crossing track in the middle of the field. Turn left to reach a stile at the field edge. Cross and maintain direction across the next two fields to reach a gap in the hedge. Go through and bear right to reach a gate and road.

Turn left to a road junction, and turn left again, following the road back through Waterperry to return to the car park.

POINTS OF INTEREST:

Waterperry House and Gardens – Although there has been a house on the site since before the days of the Doomsday Book, the current house was rebuilt in 1713 by Sir John Curson. The estate was bought by the Henley family in 1830 and was sold to Magdalen College, Oxford in 1925. In 1932 Waterperry Horticultural School was opened by Beatrix Havergal. The house is not open to the public, but the gardens are open every day except Christmas Day. Timings are: April to September : 10am – 5.30pm, October to March : 10am – 4.30pm.

St Leonard's Church, Waterstock – The earliest record of the church dates back to 1190, but it was rebuilt at the end of the 15th century. Inside there is a bust of Sir George Croke, a 17th-century judge and Lord of the Manor.

REFRESHMENTS:
The Clifden Inn, Worminghall.
There is a Tea Room at Waterperry Gardens.

NORTH AND SOUTH STOKE 7m (11$\frac{1}{4}$km)

Maps: OS Sheets Landranger 174 and 175; Pathfinder 1155; Explorer 3.

A contrasting walk along ancient tracks, through rolling countryside and a chance to visit two interesting churches.

Start: At 598835, South Stoke Church.

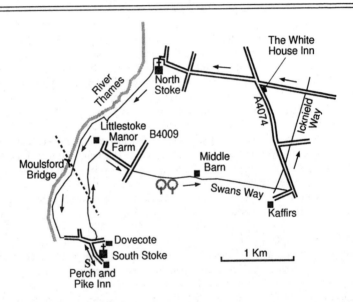

With your back to **South Stoke Church,** turn right along the road and walk to a corner. Turn right and, after 100 yards, opposite the entrance to **Manor Farm,** turn left along a footpath signed 'Little Stoke 1 mile'. On reaching a field, keep to the left edge, following a well-defined track which bends right, across the field, to reach a railway embankment. Turn left for 20 yards, then right, through a tunnel under the railway, to reach a field on the other side. Turn left to the field corner, turning right there for 25 yards before turning left through a gap in the field boundary. Bear right across the next field, following a slightly elevated footpath. Cross a bridge over a small stream and a stile, and continue ahead towards Littlestoke Manor Farm, keeping to the right of a wire fence.

At the field corner, go over a stone stile on to a road. The farm entrance is on the left. Turn right along the road, following it to reach the B4009. Cross, with care, and continue along the track opposite. The track ascends and passes a small copse on the right, and then descends to Middle Barn, before ascending again, with good views of rolling countryside. As you descend from the second rise, look out for a small post on the right, waymarked with a blue arrow. Here, turn left across the field to reach a gateway and road (the A4074). Bear left across the road, with care, and climb the embankment to reach a gateway. Bear left across the field beyond, heading towards a copse. Go through the copse (note the grave on the left) and cross a bridge to reach a road. Cross and continue along the bridleway opposite (part of the Icknield Way). On reaching the next road, turn left and follow it to its crossroads with the A4074. The White House Inn is on the left here.

Go diagonally right across the A4074, with care, and continue along the road opposite to reach the Newtown crossroads with the B4009. Cross, with care, and continue ahead along Cook Lane. The road bends right and becomes The Street: about 100 yards further on, turn left into Church Lane. Go through the lych gate and follow the path behind **North Stoke Church** tower. Leave the churchyard through a gate, following a path which bends right, then left through some interesting gardens to reach a kissing gate and field (look for the Ridgeway acorn signs). Now follow the right edge of several fields to reach the bank of the River Thames. The Ridgeway now follows the Thames towpath under **Moulsford Bridge** to reach a lane. Turn left and, on reaching the road at South Stoke, turn right to return to the church.

POINTS OF INTEREST:

St Andrew's Church, South Stoke – Cromwell stabled his horses here during the siege of Wallingford. The church is 13th century, but altered during the 14th century, though the tower is 15th century. There is a fading mural near the North Door.

Manor Farm, South Stoke – The farm includes a square four-gabled medieval brick dovecote reputed to be one of the largest in the South of England.

St Mary The Virgin Church, North Stoke – Built in about 1230-1240 the church contains some interesting 14th century wall paintings. The tower fell in 1669 and was rebuilt in 1725. The contralto Dame Clara Butt is buried in the churchyard.

Moulsford Railway Bridge – The bridge, built by Brunel in 1840, is a listed building.

REFRESHMENTS:

The Perch and Pike, South Stoke.

The White House Inn, on the A4074 to the east of Newtown.

Maps: OS Sheets Landranger 164; Pathfinder 1091 and 1068.
*A walk across fields, through part of the ancient forest of
Wychwood and along the outer boundary of the Cornbury Estate.*
Start: At 352194, Charlbury Railway Station car park.

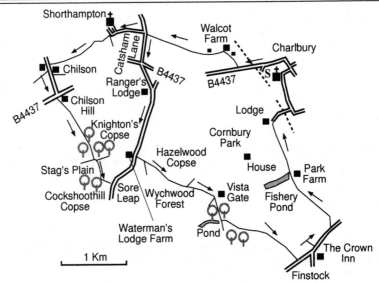

Leave the car park via the main entrance and turn left, with care, along the B4437. Go
over the railway and, after 250 yards, turn right along a bridleway signed 'Walcot
only'. You are now on the Oxfordshire Way. Just past some cottages on the right,
where the metalled track turns right to Walcot Farm, continue along a gravelled track,
passing a ruined barn. Continue along the track, which becomes grassy, to reach a
road (Catsham Lane).

   The shorter walk turns left up the road. Cross the B4437, with care, and continue
along the road opposite (signed for Leafield) to reach a road junction. Bear right, still
on the Leafield road, following it through part of the Wychwood Forest for ³/₄ mile.
Just before the entrance to Waterman's Lodge Farm, on the right, turn left over a stile,
rejoining the longer walk.

The longer walk turns right, downhill. After 20 yards, turn left along a lane signed for Shorthampton. At the first junction, with Shorthampton Church to your right, continue ahead to where the lane bends right. Here, ignore a path going left, going straight ahead, through a gate and along a farm track. Follow the track to reach a road at Chilson Farm. Turn left, through the village, continuing to reach the B4437. Turn right towards Burford. After 50 yards, turn left up a metalled track signed 'Chilson Hill only'. Go past some cottages, then ahead along a grassy track which bends left, then right, and goes along the edge of a field. At a hedge corner, turn left, and, after 30 yards, turn right along the field edge. At the far corner, go through a gap and continue with Church Brake (a copse) on your left. Go across a field and into Knighton's Copse. Walk uphill to reach a junction. Turn left and, after 20 yards, turn right. At the next junction, bear left to reach a road. Turn left, uphill, and follow the road for 600 yards to reach Waterman's Lodge Farm, on the left. Turn right over a stile, rejoining the shorter walk.

Bear right along a wide track to reach a track junction. Fork left, following yellow arrow waymarkers and going ahead at all cross-tracks, to reach the Vista Gate entrance into **Cornbury Park**. Here, veer right along a gravelled track. At a track junction, with a large pond on your right, turn left, then right, along a path which ascends quite steeply. At the next track junction, fork left. Go over at a cross-tracks, through a gate and follow the track as it leaves the forest and crosses two fields to reach the road at Finstock. Turn left, and, after 800 yards, turn left along a metalled track. Follow the track past Cornbury Park Fishery Pond, on the left, then bear right of the gate into the Park and keep to the left edge of a car park. Now follow the wrought iron boundary fence, on your left, to reach the garden of North Lodge. Go through the garden, and a gate, to reach a Park entrance. Here, turn right along the drive to reach a road. Cross, then turn left, following the road into Charlbury. At St Mary's Church, on the left, turn right to reach a T-junction. Turn left and, after 250 yards, turn left again and follow the road downhill. After 300 yards, turn left to return to Charlbury Station.

POINTS OF INTEREST:

Cornbury Park – An important part of the history of Charlbury, the house here was an Elizabethan hunting lodge given to the Earl of Leicester by Elizabeth I. It was demolished and a new house built during the reign of Charles I.

REFRESHMENTS:

The Crown Inn, Finstock.
There are numerous opportunities in Charlbury.

Walk 98   **WINDSOR GREAT PARK** $7^1/_4$m ($11^1/_2$km)

Maps: OS Sheets Landranger 175; Pathfinder 1173.

A pleasant walk through Windsor Great Park, ambling over the boundary into Surrey to visit the well-known Savill Gardens.

Start: At 961743, the car park on the eastern side of the A332 in Windsor Great Park.

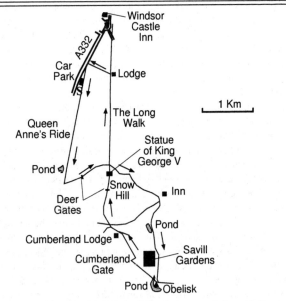

With your back to the A332, and with Windsor Castle to your left, walk forward to reach a wide ride (Queen Anne's Ride). Turn right and follow the ride, ascending gently to reach a metalled drive. Turn left and follow the drive, passing a turning on the right to reach a gate in the Deer Park fence. Go through the pedestrian gate on the right and continue along the drive. After 700 yards you reach the Long Walk, on your left, and a good view of Windsor Castle. Continue along the drive as it bends to the right, crossing a small bridge to reach another gate in the Deer Park fence. Go through and walk ahead to reach the drive of the Royal Lodge, on your right. Here, turn left towards Bishopgate Lodge. About 30 yards before you reach the lodge, bear right across a grassy area to reach a green wooden gate in the hedge. Go through and turn right along an enclosed track. Ignore a track going off to the left, continuing straight on and, shortly, on the right, you will see Cow Pond. This is a pleasant place to stop to admire the ducks. Continuing along the Rhododendron Ride, created by George IV, the track is soon joined by a gravelled track joining from the right. The **Savill Gardens** are now ahead, to the right. Keep ahead for a further 200 yards to arrive at the entrance to the Gardens. The walk continues past the Garden entrance to reach the **Obelisk**, and Obelisk Pond, on the right.

Turn sharp right along another ride, following it downhill, over an ornate bridge, and up the other side. Over to your left are the polo playing fields of Smith's Lawn. Go past some cottages, on the right, and continue to a tarmac drive. Turn right through Cumberland Gate. About 20 yards after passing Cumberland Lodge, turn left along a faint path across a grassy area. Cross the drive to Cumberland Lodge, on your left, and bear slightly left to reach a drive junction. Maintain direction across the drive, going down a track just opposite. On your right is the boundary fence of the Royal Lodge, and, on your left, is Ox Pond. Go past a barrier, and along a wide enclosed track. Go over at a cross-tracks, where you have a good view of the Royal Lodge to your right. Go through a gate in the Deer Park fence and follow the path beyond fairly steeply uphill to reach the **Copper Horse** statue.

You are now standing at the highest point of the Great Park. From here there is not only an excellent view of Windsor Castle, but also of the surrounding area, including Heathrow Airport on a clear day. Facing the castle, leave the Copper Horse by dropping down to the Long Ride. Follow the ride to reach the pedestrian gate at Park Pale Lodge. Go through and turn left through a second gate. Continue ahead to reach the A332 and turn left to return to the car park.

POINTS OF INTEREST:

Savill Gardens – This 35 acre woodland garden was started in 1932. It provides beauty and interest all the year round. It has set opening times and there is an admission charge. However, entry to the tearooms is free.

Obelisk – The obelisk was erected by George II as a present to his son.

Copper Horse – The horse is an equestrian statue of George III. It was erected by George IV. It stands at the highest point of the 4800 acres of Windsor Great Park.

REFRESHMENTS:

There are a number of inns and refreshment places in Windsor. The tearooms in the Savill Gardens are open whenever the gardens are open.

Walk 99   THAME $7\frac{1}{4}$m ($11\frac{1}{2}$km)

Maps: OS Sheets Landranger 165; Explorer 2.

A fairly level walk across Thame Park to the village of Sydenham.

Start: At 711053, the Four Horseshoes Inn, Thame.

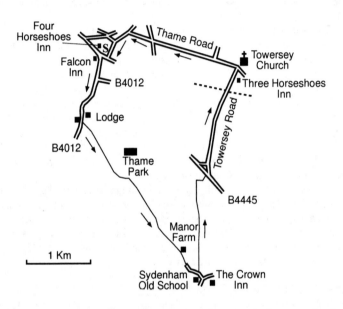

Parking is possible in the side road close to the inn. If you use the inn car park, please check with the landlord beforehand. With your back to the inn, turn left and take the right-hand fork, Thame Park Road (the B4012) towards Postcombe. Go over the railway line and continue along the road, with care, for $\frac{1}{2}$ mile, to reach an arched entrance into Thame Park on the left. Continue for another 150 yards, then turn left over a stile. Bear right across Thame Park, passing just to the left of the first tree on the right and looking out for well-spaced out direction posts. When you are parallel with Thame Park House, on the left, go over a drive and bear slightly right along a path to reach a fence stile and footbridge. Cross and bear diagonally left across a field to reach another bridge in the far left-hand corner. Cross the bridge and bear diagonally right across New Park, following the direction of the arrows on the waymarker posts. At the far

188

corner, bear left along a farm track. Go through a gap and along a field edge. The Chilterns can be seen ahead here. Go through a gateway and bear right down a farm track. Ahead, and to the right, you can seen the radio mast at Stokenchurch.

At the bottom of the track, cross a stile, just to the left of a gate. The entrance to a house called 'The Tays' is on the right: here, turn left along a metalled track, passing to the right of some barns. Go over a cattle grid and continue, passing Manor Farm on your right. After another 100 yards, when you reach a row of houses, look for a signed footpath on the left. Keep this in mind as you will be returning to this point. Continue along the lane to reach a T-junction. **Sydenham Old School Room** is on the right, and the Crown Inn is just across the road, also to the right. From the T-junction, retrace your steps and turn right along the path seen earlier, going between houses. Cross a stile and bear left, then right across a field. Go over a stile by a telegraph pole, and cross the field beyond. At the far side, go over another stile and straight across the garden of a cottage. Cross a stile and go across the middle of the field beyond. Go through a gateway, then along the right edge of two fields. Just before the far corner, turn right over a stile, then immediately turn left along a field edge. At the next corner, turn right and, after 100 yards, bear left across a bridge.

Go across the field beyond to reach the B4445. Cross, with care, and go over a grassy strip to reach another road. Turn left to reach a road junction. Bear right along a road signed 'Towersey 1', following it for a mile to reach a road junction. St Catherine's Church is opposite, on the right. Turn left along Thame Road, following it to its junction with the B4012. Cross, with care, and continue along Towersey Road opposite. Pass a school, on the left, to reach a road junction. Turn left and, at the second turning on the right (Kings Road), turn right. At the next junction, turn left along East Street. At the far end, at a mini-roundabout, if you want to visit **Thame**, turn right. Otherwise, turn left and follow the road back to the Four Horseshoes Inn.

POINTS OF INTEREST:

Sydenham Old School Room – Built originally in 1849, and enlarged in 1886, the school catered for the village children. It closed in 1949 and is now used as a village hall. The plaque on the wall states that the community is recorded in the Doomsday Book. The name Sydenham means 'by the wide river meadow'.

Thame – The town dates back to the 12th century. An agricultural show and fair, one of the largest in the country, are held here every September.

REFRESHMENTS:

The Crown Inn, Sydenham.
There are numerous opportunities in Thame, including those mentioned in the text.

THE ROLLRIGHT STONES $7^1/_2$m (12km)
Maps: OS Sheets Landranger 164 and 151, Pathfinder 1068 and 1044.

A walk across fields to the site of a mythical story about a proud king, his men, and his whispering knights.

Start: At 313271, the car park near Chipping Norton Town Hall.

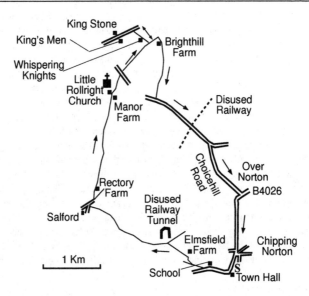

From the car park, head towards the town hall and turn right down New Street (the A44). Go past the entrance to Penshurst School and, after 30 yards, turn right into a Recreation Ground. Turn left and follow the path signed 'Salford $1^1/_2$'. Go through a swing gate just to the left of an enclosed play area, and bear right down a field. Cross a bridge at the bottom of a dip, and bear right up a field towards houses. Cross a stile to the left of the houses, go across a drive and over the stile opposite. Go up the next field to reach a stile in the right-hand corner. Go over and along the right edge of a field to its corner. Swing left and, after 25 yards, turn right over a stile, and go along the right edge of the next field. Go over a stile in the far corner, and turn left along the field edge, walking with a hedge on your left. At the far side the path becomes enclosed between hedgerows: Cross a stone bridge and go along a narrow path, with Christmas trees on the right, to reach a house on the right.

Go through a gate, along a drive, and then along a road. Where the road bends left to the village green, turn right down a lane, signed 'Trout Lakes – Rectory Farm'. Ignore the first path on the left, continuing to reach an avenue of poplars. Here, turn left over a stile and bear diagonally right across a field, aiming to the left of Rectory Farm. Cross a stile and, after 5 yards, bear left to reach a stile in field corner. Cross and go along the right edge of a field, cutting a corner to reach a stile at the edge of a small wood. Cross and follow path through the wood. At the far side, go through a gate and along the edge of a field. At the far field corner, turn right through a gate, then left along the field edge. At the next corner go through a gap, and cross a stream and a farm track, to the path opposite. Bear left up the narrow path through trees and, at the far side, go through a gate and along the left edge of a field. Cross a stile just right of the far corner, then ahead across the middle of a field, descending to Manor Farm. Go between barns to reach a road.

Turn left and, after 30 yards turn right up the edge of a field. When the garden on the left ends, go up the middle of the field and, at the top, cross a road, and go along the track opposite. When the track ends, go along the right edge of a field, then across the middle of the next field. To visit the **Rollright Stones**, turn left along the field edge, passing the Whispering Knights, on the left, to reach a road. Turn left to reach, after 250 yards, the King Stone on your right. After another 25 yards, on the left, is the entrance to the King's Men Stone Circle. Now retrace your steps to the Whispering Knights and continue along the field edge. After 150 yards, turn left over a stile and cross a field to reach a farm track. Turn right. Go to the left of Brighthill Farm to reach a stile. Bear right down the field beyond to cross another stile in the far right corner. Go down the edge of the next field, cross a stile in the bottom corner and bear right along the right edge of two fields to reach a road. Turn left to a road junction and fork right to Over Norton. At the T-junction, turn right and follow the B4026 around a sharp left-hand bend, using the pavement on the left to return to Chipping Norton.

POINTS OF INTEREST:
Rollright Stones - The Whispering Knights, the oldest of the stones, are a portal dolmen burial chamber. The King's Men form an almost perfect circle about 36 yards in diameter. The circle is thought to be late Neolithic or early Bronze Age. The King Stone is thought to be a different age to the other stones.

REFRESHMENTS:
There are ample opportunities in Chipping Norton.

TITLES IN THE SERIES